Dear Jarron,

I just want to know "the 300 plus
that I now
finger of the So
ordinances in the
2021. Let's just say
that quickly, the mysteries
Things I never would have learn. The scriptures
wise have opened up to me. The
Holy Ghost guides me through not just those
are patterned + multi-dimensional. The
aspects but he knows exactly when each
account of the Bible + Book of Mormon
were written. He lines them up in
chronological order for me to understand
them, something I could never have
done without the spirit. The symbolism
is amazing when he explains it to you,
it fills the gaps of all the others. The
Book of Mormon is true 100%. Joseph
Smith did see God the Father + His Son
Jesus Christ. Someday I hope you will
know how I helped in the gathering +
a little something called "Operation
Many" but it will come in the
Lord's time. Love you,
Mom

12-6-22

The
PARABLES
of JESUS

The PARABLES *of* JESUS

MIRRORS *to the* SOUL, WINDOWS *to* ETERNITY

GERALD N. LUND

DESERET
BOOK

SALT LAKE CITY, UTAH

Library of Congress Cataloging-in-Publication Data

(CIP on file)

ISBN 978-1-63993-075-3

Printed in the United States of America
Lake Book Manufacturing, Inc., Melrose Park, IL

10 9 8 7 6 5 4 3 2 1

Contents

PART IV: PREPARATION FOR CHRIST'S COMING

Preface

As I write this preface, we are quickly approaching the end of a second year of the global pandemic known as COVID-19. In these last two years we have seen much change, much upheaval, much erosion of the values we hold dear, and much uncertainty about what the future holds for us. Across the world we are seeing high anxiety about how to prepare ourselves and those we love for such turbulent times. How do we cope with these ground-shifting challenges?

I am often asked where I get ideas for the books I choose to write and how I choose one particular topic over another as my next project.

There are, of course, many things that factor into those decisions. And the reasons for starting on a book of fiction are different than the reasons for starting on a doctrinal book. In the case of doctrinal books, it often comes from something I have been teaching in a class or perhaps at a devotional.

The beginning of this book goes back many years. While in Southern California teaching institute for the Church Educational System, I enrolled at Pepperdine University to do some graduate studies in the New Testament. Like BYU, Pepperdine University is a private university with a direct religious affiliation. It is owned by the Churches of Christ, a conservative Christian group in the United States.

I already had completed a master's degree in sociology at Brigham Young University, but when I chose a career with CES, I desired to do further work in Bible studies. So while I didn't necessarily need another degree, I enrolled at Pepperdine, taking one or two classes each semester one day a week. It turned out to be a wonderful learning experience for the next three years. Not only were the professors deeply committed Christians, but what I most appreciated about my experience was that they taught us both *about* the New Testament and *how to study* the Bible so as to draw out its fuller meaning and the power of its message.

Even in my first years as a seminary teacher, I had come to love the New Testament. And part of that love centered around the parables that Jesus taught. The same time I was in California and doing my studies at Pepperdine, I also wrote my first book, a book on prophecy and the Second Coming. A couple of years later, while still at Pepperdine, I began my first book of fiction. And it was in that turn to fiction that I began to take particular notice of the parables.

What I discovered was that the parables are what I shall call miniature "literary masterpieces." Most of them are brief, some just a few verses. And yet in that brevity we find a strong story structure, vivid characterizations, and simple but profound moral lessons that deeply touch the soul. Over and over I noticed how the Savior captured in a sentence—and sometimes in a single word—a wonderful insight into a person's character and beliefs.

Over the years I have taught classes on the New Testament, and especially classes on the parables. Those experiences have only served to increase my appreciation for their literary structure, deepen my love for the lessons they teach, and intensify my profound appreciation for the Teacher who created them, even Jesus Christ, our Savior, Redeemer, and Exemplar.

MIRRORS TO THE SOUL

It seemed clear from the beginning that the title for this book should be called *The Parables of Jesus*. But I felt like it also needed a secondary title, something that captured why the parables have so much value for each of us. After some thought, I decided that "Mirrors to the Soul" captured what I was feeling. I liked that imagery because in my own experience, over and over as I pondered on this parable or that, I found myself putting myself into those simple yet profound stories. It was like I was holding up a "mirror" and studying my own reflection.

In the Upper Room, the night before He died, Jesus surprised the Twelve when He sadly announced that one of them there would betray Him. Matthew records: "And they were exceeding sorrowful, and began every one of them to say unto him, *Lord, is it I?*" (Matthew 26:22; emphasis added). It says much about their character that their first response to that shocking announcement was not to look around the room and point fingers at the others, but to look inward at their own hearts.

Ironically, Judas was there that night too. He had already committed himself to the Sanhedrin to deliver Jesus to them for thirty pieces of silver. So those words must have shocked him deeply. But he couldn't reveal that, of course. To cover his own perfidy, he too asked, "Lord, is it I?" Jesus answered with three simple words: "Thou hast said" (Matthew 26:25).

I have come to believe that this is one of the primary reasons why Jesus taught in parables. These simple but powerful stories hold up a mirror and give us an opportunity to take a good, long look at ourselves and ask: "Lord, is it I?"

Here is just one example of how the parables become like a mirror. We think of the story of the good Samaritan and ask ourselves this question: "If I had been one of those traveling on the road to Jericho that day, would I have stopped to help the man who had been attacked by thieves, or would I too have crossed to the other side of the road, pretending not to see him, and hurried on?" It is sobering to realize that if we are really honest, the answer might not be to our liking.

This process of self-assessment that comes as we study ourselves in the mirror can be an intensely uncomfortable or deeply enlightening and spiritually invigorating experience.

WINDOWS TO ETERNITY

Then one day another thought came to me. "Isn't there more to these scriptural jewels than one's own self-evaluation?" The answer came quickly and clearly. "Of course." The parables not only teach us what Jesus expects of us; they also teach us *the very nature of Jesus Himself, and through Him, the nature of our Father in Heaven.*

Christ has taught: "I would that ye should be perfect *even as I, or your Father who is in heaven is perfect*" (3 Nephi 12:48; emphasis added). And in that sense, the parables are like mirrors that help us examine ourselves and strive more diligently to live as Jesus lives. But in another way, they are like windows we can look out to see the greater vision of God's perfect nature, the deeper insights that come from the Savior's teachings, and the broader scope of God's eternal plan of happiness.

It's like we are walking in a dark hallway and suddenly we come to a window that looks out on the world. We are stunned to see how much more there is out there than just our narrow little corridor.

If we are inspired by the unselfish love of the good Samaritan and strive to be more like him, how much more do we come to understand the perfect character and attributes of the Savior, who gave us the parable? And if that is so, how much more does our love of the Father deepen?

To put it another way: the teachings of Jesus, including the parables, provide a powerful incentive to know more, live better, love deeper, and strive to become more like the Father and the Son. In a mirror, we have the opportunity to study ourselves. Through windows, we have the opportunity to see what is outside ourselves, including the plan of our Father for His children. Both are apt metaphors for the parables of Jesus.

This book does not attempt to examine every parable that Jesus taught during His earthly ministry. That is beyond its scope. What you will find here are parables which, in the estimation of the author, provide some of the best mirrors and the best windows into our lives.

One last question to keep in mind as you consider these parables: Which is the greater—the story or the author who writes it? Clearly, the value of the parables of Jesus is that they teach us more about Jesus! Two of the major things the parables teach us are *how* to live and how *not* to live in order to find joy. In other words, they provide an opportunity for us to take a long and thoughtful look at who we are and where we are going.

In His great Intercessory Prayer that Jesus offered to His Father shortly before His death, He summarized what our goal in this life should be: "And this is life eternal, that they might know thee the only true God, and Jesus Christ, whom thou hast sent" (John 17:3).

Moroni closed out the Book of Mormon record by describing how it is that we human beings living in a fallen world can achieve that ultimate goal: "Come unto Christ, and *be perfected in him*, and deny yourselves of all ungodliness; and if ye shall deny yourselves of all ungodliness, and love God with all your might, mind and strength, *then is his grace sufficient for you, that by his grace ye may be perfect in Christ*" (Moroni 10:32; emphasis added).

Think of the parables of Jesus as providing practical insights and guidelines into that process of moving toward perfection. Christ, through His Infinite Atonement, is the *promise* of eternal joy. The parables of Jesus are both *mirrors to our souls* and *windows into eternity* that help us achieve that promise.

Gerald N. Lund
Alpine, Utah
January 1, 2022

Imagery, Symbolism, *and* Parables

In the book of Moses, Enoch recorded how Adam and Eve were taught by the Lord about the ordinance of baptism. They were the first humans to ever hear that concept and the doctrine that lies behind it. After telling them that this was a required gospel ordinance for entry into the kingdom of God, the Lord then made an interesting comparison. He likened being "born again" into the kingdom of God to our birth into this world.

> Behold, *all things* have their likeness, and *all things are created and made to bear record of me*, both things which are *temporal*, and things which are *spiritual*; things which are *in the heavens above*, and things which are *on the earth*, and things which are *in the earth*, and things which are *under the earth*, both above and beneath: *all things bear record of me*. (Moses 6:63; emphasis added)

What the Lord called a "likeness" is what we more commonly call imagery and symbolic language. But in that verse, He clearly states that the things of this world can teach us eternal truths. We know that symbolic language permeates all of our scriptures, but especially in the Old and New Testaments. This should not surprise us, for imagery and symbolism were part of everyday life in the times of Jesus. That is the case in some cultures more than others. And the peoples of the Bible were part of those cultures.

I point this out because the parables of Jesus come from the New Testament, which was written by people of the Middle East about two thousand years ago. And their culture, in some ways, was very different from modern Western culture. Here is an interesting observation from a scholar of Middle Eastern studies on the implication of that statement:

> We ofttimes read our Bible as though its peoples were English or American and interpret their sayings in terms of our own background and psychology. But the Bible is actually an [Eastern][1] book. It was written centuries ago by [Eastern] people and primarily for [Eastern] people. . . . It may be of interest to contrast the speech of modern and ancient Palestinians with our own. In thought and speech the [Eastern person] is an artist; the [Western person], on the other hand, may be thought of as an architect. When speaking, the [Eastern person] paints a scene whose total effect is true, but the details may be inaccurate; the [Western person] tends to draw diagrams accurate in detail. (Sidney B. Sperry, "Hebrew Manners and Customs," *Ensign*, May 1972)

Another Latter-day Saint expert in the Middle East put it this way:

> Western readers expect a text to contain a meaning that is fully expressed and immediately understood. Eastern peoples, in general, love verbal symbolism that must be pondered and savored. The revealed phrase is for them an array of symbols from which more and more flashes of spiritual awareness come with each reading. The words are reference points for an inexhaustible doctrine, the implicit meaning

is everything, and the obscurities of the literal meaning are so many veils masking the majesty of the content. (James B. Mayfield, "Ishmael, Our Brother," *Ensign,* June 1979)

This article was written over forty years ago now, and much has changed in the Middle East since that time. East and West are more similar in many ways now. However, the Eastern tendency to use imagery and symbolism is still found there, especially away from the large cities where the people still maintain much of their traditional culture.

The parables found in the Old and New Testaments are excellent examples of this deeply rooted ancient love of "likening" things in our lives with things found in nature. And we also have to keep in mind that the parables of Jesus are not the product of the modern Middle East, but the ancient one. Thus, the symbolic imagery and language of that day permeate the language of the parables, and if we ignore that, we will miss much of the richness of these parables.

Though some symbolism can be esoteric, with only a small group of people with specialized knowledge understanding it, much of the Bible symbolism is easily discerned with some reflection because the peoples of those cultures drew from things from their everyday lives that we understand well. Therefore, in seeking interpretations for this language, we can ask ourselves, "What was it about the nature of this object that caused people to draw likenesses from it?"

One other consideration is of value as we discuss how to better interpret scriptural symbolism and apply it to our day. This counsel was given to us by the Prophet Joseph Smith:

I make this broad declaration that whenever God gives a vision of an image, or beast, or figure of any kind, *he always holds Himself responsible to give a revelation or interpretation of the meaning thereof,* otherwise we are not responsible or accountable for our belief in it. Don't be afraid of being damned for not knowing the meaning of a vision or figure if God has not given a revelation or interpretation of the subject. ("History, 1838–1856, volume D-1 [1 August 1842–1 July 1843]," p. 1523, *The Joseph Smith Papers*, accessed January 30, 2022, https://www.josephsmithpapers .org/paper-summary/history-1838-1856-volume-d-1-1 -august-1842-1-july-1843/166; emphasis added)

We shall follow that counsel throughout this book.

SCRIPTURAL SYMBOLISM AND THE PARABLES OF JESUS

Why do I take this much time to talk about scriptural symbolism in a book on the parables of Jesus? Because these parables come from, and are deeply rooted in, that rich Eastern heritage. Within them we find various layers of meaning and application to our lives today.

Like other forms of symbolism, the parables were designed to (1) bring enlightenment and truth to those who seek it; and (2) yet appear to be nothing more than charming stories or similes to those who are not as prepared spiritually. When Jesus first taught in parables, the Twelve were taken aback by this approach. Afterward, when they were alone with Him, they asked: "Why speakest thou unto them in parables?" His answer is a reminder to us all:

Who hath ears to hear, let him hear. . . . Therefore speak I to them in parables: because *they seeing see not*, and *hearing they hear not, neither do they understand.* And in them is fulfilled the prophecy of Esaias, which saith, By hearing ye shall hear, and shall not understand; and seeing ye shall see, and shall not perceive. For this people's heart is waxed gross, and their ears are dull of hearing, and their eyes they have closed; lest at any time they should see with their eyes, and hear with their ears, and should understand with their heart, and should be converted, and I should heal them. (Matthew 13:10, 13–15; emphasis added)

To put it simply, the remarkable thing about symbolism and imagery in the scriptures, in all of its forms, including parables, is that it can both *reveal* and *conceal* meaning simultaneously, depending on the openness of the hearts of the listeners. While one listener might be deeply touched and say, "I believe," another walks away, shaking his head.

The word *parable* in the New Testament is a word translated from the Greek *parabollo*. This comes from the prefix *para*—"to place alongside," as in *para*llel—and *bolay*—"to throw or hurl," as in our word *balli*stics. One Bible scholar defined the word as meaning "to lay side by side; to compare; to place one thing beside another" (*Unger's Bible Dictionary*, 823).

The word in the Old Testament translated as parable means "to be like" or "sentences constructed in parallels" (James Hastings, *Dictionary of the Bible*, 678).

The Book of Mormon makes no mention of parables, but the allegory of the olive trees (Jacob 5) is actually an extensive parable with that same parabolic structure. It is interesting that in the Doctrine and Covenants, "parable" is found about fifty times. Many of those are references to Bible parables. Some are modern parables that Joseph Smith received from the Savior.

In the Bible Dictionary, which is included with Latter-day Saint printings of the Bible, there is an entry on parables that provides some very helpful insights:

The parable conveys to the hearer religious truth *exactly in proportion to his faith and intelligence*; to the dull and uninspired it is a mere story, "seeing they see not," while to the instructed and spiritual it reveals the mysteries or secrets of the kingdom of heaven. Thus it is that the parable exhibits the condition for finding true knowledge. *Only he who seeks finds.* . . .

It is important to distinguish between the *interpretation* of a parable and the *application* of a parable. The only true interpretation is the meaning the parable conveyed, or was meant to convey, when first spoken. The application of a parable may vary in every age and circumstance. But if the original meaning is to be grasped, *it is important to consider its context and setting.* The thought to which it is linked, the connection in which it is placed, the persons to whom it is addressed, all give the clue to the right interpretation. (Bible Dictionary, 740–41; emphasis added)

The Prophet Joseph Smith made a similar recommendation: "I have a key by which I understand the scriptures. I enquire, what was the question which drew out the answer, or caused Jesus to utter the parable? . . . To ascertain its meaning, we must dig up the root and ascertain what it was that drew the saying out of Jesus" (*Discourses*, 253).

A recent and very thorough scholarly work on the parables by a Christian scholar made these observations about the parables:

The parables make up about thirty-five per cent of Jesus' teachings in the Synoptic[2] [gospels]. . . . There are relatively few parables in Mark. . . . For the rest of the parables, ten are unique to Matthew and eighteen are unique to Luke. About two thirds of the parables are in Luke. (Klyne Snodgrass, *Stories with Intent: A Comprehensive Guide to the Parables of Jesus,* 22–23)

This same scholar lists various characteristics of the parables of Jesus. This helps us better understand why they are important to us. Here are some items he notes:

- The parables of Jesus are, first of all, brief. Thirty-three of them have four verses or less.
- Parables are marked by simplicity and symmetry.
- Jesus's parables are mostly about people.
- Most of them are drawn from everyday life.
- The parables are engaging; they hold our attention.
- The lesson or most crucial part of the parable is usually at the end of the parable.
- In most cases, the parable is set in a specific context.
- Most of the parables teach us about the nature of God and what it means to be a true disciple.

THE PARABLES OF JESUS IN THIS WORK

My purpose in this book is not to present an exhaustive study of the parables of Jesus. The subtitle of this book illustrates my purpose, which is to use the parables to gain better insight into our lives and from that draw closer to Christ. There are numerous New Testament parables that have not been analyzed here. Partly that is due to space. Partly that is because the parables I have chosen seem to best help us achieve this purpose: to see these parables as both mirrors to our souls and windows to eternity.

The format for our study is the same throughout the book. Each chapter has four sections:

- Context and setting
- The parable

- Analysis
- Application

In addition, I have grouped the parables we shall study in this book into four categories or themes. Each is its own section of the book. Each provides insights into the theme for that group. However, some parables carry multiple applications and could easily be placed in more than one category. So I chose to put them where I felt the emphasis was stronger. These categories are:

- Part I: Our Relationship with Deity
- Part II: Gospel Application
- Part III: Ministering
- Part IV: Preparation for Christ's Coming

I shall close with a wonderful description of the value of the parables in our day. It was given some years ago by Virginia U. Jensen, who was serving as the First Counselor in the Relief Society General Presidency at the time.

> When Jesus lived on the earth he taught using uncomplicated words and stories that all could understand, knowing that open hearts would receive the full impact of his message. His sermons and parables provide elegantly simple instructions that we might compare to a mountain climber's tools: They are compact, multipurpose, and applicable to any number of possible situations. We can distill from the New Testament a selection of these tools to carry in our spiritual backpacks as we hike the steep and rocky, as well as the smooth, trails of our earthly excursion. ("I Can Do All Things Through Christ," *The Best of Women's Conferences*, 228–29)

And with that introduction, let us now begin our study of the parables of Jesus.

NOTES

1. The author originally used the words *Oriental* and *Occidental* to distinguish between Eastern and Western peoples. Language has been modernized.

2. *Synoptic* means "with the same general view." Matthew, Mark, and Luke are known as the Synoptic gospels because each of them focuses primarily on the life and teachings of Jesus, whereas John's gospel seems to assume that his readers have those other gospels and his focus is on more of the doctrine that Christ taught both by word and example.

Part I

Our Relationship
with Deity

Chapter 1

Laborers *in the* Vineyard

CONTEXT AND SETTING

What drew this parable forth from the Savior is quite clear. From Matthew's description in chapter 19, this seems to have been a typical day when Jesus was teaching and interacting with the multitudes. Then a young man approached Jesus and asked, "Good Master, what good thing shall I do, that I shall have eternal life?"

That is a commendable question and showed that the young man was seeking to improve himself. Jesus gently suggested that there was only one good person, which was God Himself, then added, "But if thou will enter into life, keep the commandments." The young man responded with one word: "Which?"

Think about that question. Though it seems at first to be a good response, closer consideration suggests something else. Though he may not have intended it in this way, by asking which of the commandments he was required to keep, in a way wasn't the young man at the same time asking which commandments he could ignore and not worry about?

Jesus answered his question by quickly citing some of the Ten Commandments—murder, adultery, theft, bearing false witness, honoring parents. Then He added a commandment that was not part of the original ten, but was added by Moses in the book of Leviticus: "Thou shalt love thy neighbor as thyself" (Leviticus 19:18).

The young man's response was immediate, and reveals that he had a pretty high opinion of himself: "All these things have I kept from my youth up; What lack I yet?"

One is strongly tempted to say, "A little humility." But Jesus responded with something that must have shocked the young man deeply. "If thou wilt be perfect, go and sell that thou hast, and give to the poor, and thou shalt have treasure in heaven: and come and follow me."

Matthew then recorded: "But when the young man heard that saying, he went away sorrowful: for he had great possessions" (Matthew 19:16–22).

Jesus then turned to the disciples[1] and said: "Verily I say unto you, That a rich man shall hardly enter into the kingdom of heaven. And again I say unto you, It is easier for a camel to go through the eye of an needle, than for a rich man to enter into the kingdom of God" (Matthew 19:23–24).

A side note here is in order. It is believed by some that Jesus's reference to the eye of a needle in describing the difficulty of a rich man getting into heaven actually referred to a small opening in the walls surrounding Jerusalem. However, it is much more likely that it is what we call hyperbole. Hyperbole is the deliberate exaggeration of something to make a point, and such exaggeration is common in the culture and rhetorical language of the Middle East, as it is in Western cultures.

Dummelow says of this erroneous idea: "Some have thought (but it seems without sufficient authority) that the 'eye of the needle' is a term applied to a small gate for foot passengers, situated at the side of large city gate through which a camel would naturally pass" (Dummelow: 689–90).

But whether or not there was such a gate, the hyperbole is clear, and the Savior's statement clearly shocked His disciples: "When his disciples heard it, they were exceedingly amazed, saying, Who then can be saved? But Jesus beheld them, and said unto them, With men, this is impossible; but with God all things are possible" (Matthew 19:25–26).

That this instruction may have been only for the Twelve is suggested by the fact that it is Peter who then asked: "Behold, we [the Twelve?] have forsaken all, and followed thee; what shall we have therefore?" (Matthew 19:27). Also note the use of the number twelve in the Savior's answer. This time, Jesus answered him forthrightly and with a marvelous promise.

> Verily, I say unto you, That ye which have followed me, in the regeneration[2] when the Son of man shall sit in the throne of his glory, ye also shall sit upon twelve thrones, judging the twelve tribes of Israel. And every one that hath forsaken houses, or brethren, or sisters, or father, or mother, or wife, or children, or lands, for my name's sake, shall receive an hundredfold, and shall inherit everlasting life. But many that are first shall be last; and the last shall be first. (Matthew 19:27–30)

Note especially His closing statement about the first and the last. It is not clear here what that means, especially for those to whom He was speaking. But the promise of eternal life is clear. And with that promise ringing in their hearts, Jesus immediately launched into the parable, which begins in chapter 20.

THE PARABLE

For the kingdom of heaven is like unto a man that is an householder [i.e., master of the house], which went out early in the morning to hire labourers into his vineyard. And when he had agreed with the labourers for a penny a day, he sent them into his vineyard.

And he went out about the third hour, and saw others standing idle in the marketplace,

And said unto them; Go ye also into the vineyard, and whatsoever is right I will give you. And they went their way.

Again he went out about the sixth and ninth hour, and did likewise.

And about the eleventh hour he went out, and found others standing idle, and saith unto them, Why stand ye here all the day idle? They say unto him, Because no man hath hired us. He saith unto them, Go ye also into the vineyard; and whatsoever is right, that shall ye receive.

So when even was come, the lord of the vineyard saith unto his steward, Call the labourers, and give them their hire, beginning from the last unto the first. And when they came that were hired about the eleventh hour, they received every man a penny. But when the first came, they supposed that they should have received more; and they likewise received every man a penny.

And when they had received it, they murmured against the goodman of the house, Saying, These last have wrought but one hour, and thou hast made them equal unto us, which have borne the burden and heat of the day.

But he answered one of them, and said, Friend, I do thee no wrong: didst not thou agree with me for a penny? Take that thine is, and go thy way: I will give unto this last, even as unto thee. Is it not lawful for me to do what I will with mine own? Is thine eye evil, because I am good?

So the last shall be first, and the first last: for many be called, but few chosen. (Matthew 20:1–16)

ANALYSIS

This is one of the longer of the many parables Jesus taught during His ministry. And, as was often the case with His parables, it opens with the phrase, "For the kingdom of heaven is like unto. . . ." That seems to indicate that Jesus isn't just teaching the people random gospel concepts or giving them a simple set of rules for daily living. He's teaching eternal principles that lead us to eternal life—the life on which the young man of great wealth had just turned his back and gone away sorrowing.

I note again that Jesus ended His previous conversation with the disciples with a sober warning: "But many that are first shall be last; and the last shall be first" (Matthew 19:30). Now, He closed the parable with that same admonition to the young man (see Matthew 20:16).

To better appreciate this parable we need to more fully understand the customs in the Middle East at the time of Jesus. Back then in many places there were what we now call "day laborers." These were men who were not hired on a permanent basis by one employer. Most towns and cities had a public square where people gathered for a specific purpose—to indicate that they were available for employment for the day, or longer if needed. Anyone who needed temporary help could then come to the square where the laborers congregated and hire the help they needed.

Remember, by this point, Jesus was not speaking to the rich young man any longer. He was speaking to His disciples, and possibly specifically to the Twelve. He had already told them that "many that are first shall be last; and the last shall be first." First in what? Last in what? The Lord doesn't say here, but it may help if we look more closely at the elements of the parable.

Remember that the word *parable* means to place things side by side in a parallel structure so as to teach or illustrate a point. With that in mind, throughout this book I shall utilize that structure to make comparisons that can help us better understand the key items from the parable. The hope is to draw gospel lessons from the parables and apply them in our own lives as we seek to bring our lives more in harmony with the will of God so that we can have His blessings, especially the blessing of inspiration and revelation through the Holy Ghost. Without this, we cannot be fully effective in our quest for exaltation and in doing the work required of us to help build up kingdom of God.

In the structure below, the first column contains a specific element from the parable. The second column suggests possible parallels in our lives that help us understand the gospel principles that Jesus is trying to teach. Remember this point, however. The elements in the parable may have multiple meanings and applications, even for the same person. The interpretations that follow will be only one of the possibilities the Spirit may choose to give to various individuals. Therefore, readers are strongly encouraged to study and ponder on these wonderful stories and pray for the enlightening gifts of the Spirit—both general principles and specific personal direction—to understand the parable more fully, for each was given to us to instruct us on what the Father and the Son would have us know and do. With that in mind, let us look more closely at some possible meanings of the key elements of the parable:

The vineyard	A metaphor for the world that serves as the home for all the human family. This also implies that all of God's children are invited—or will at some time in their eternal progression be invited—to labor in His vineyard.
The householder, or foreman	The Father and/or His Son. They who direct the work of the kingdom throughout the world through the influence of the Holy Ghost.
Early morning	In the more general sense, this probably suggests the earlier dispensations of the gospel. But on a more personal level, some of us are born into the covenant while others may not find the gospel until late in their lives.
Hiring of first laborers	In a historic sense, this could go back as far as Adam and Eve, Enoch, Abraham, Moses, etc. All were called early in the history of the world. But there can also be a personal interpretation. Some are born into a family that has been in the Church for generations. Others may be the first in their families. Some may find the gospel in their teens while others not until much later in life. Some may come into the kingdom in its earliest stages, while others find it when it is a worldwide organization. The point is that all are called to the same work.
What "I will give you" (v. 4)	These are the promised blessings for serving in the work of the Lord, both temporal and spiritual, and both temporal and eternal blessings.

Hires more laborers (third, sixth, ninth hours)	Later in history in different dispensations or later in life. The key is that they were "hired" to join in the work.
Standing idle later in the day	Those who didn't have an opportunity to hear the gospel and be invited to join in the work earlier.
Evening, the eleventh hour	Near the end of the "day," most likely our times, i.e., the dispensation of the fullness of times. But also the call comes later in life.
"Whatsoever is right" (v. 7)	God will bless all who serve as He sees fit. But these may not be only general blessings given to all, but the numerous individual blessings that come from God.
The heat of the day	This seems to be a metaphorical reference to the tests and challenges that come with living the gospel and from life itself. And here too, this "heat" can vary from the normal challenges of life to severe persecution or prolonged, debilitating challenges. In some cases these have led to martyrdom.
All receive the same reward	That reward is ultimately the possibility of gaining eternal life with God and Christ, through the plan of happiness and the infinite power of the Atonement of Jesus Christ. Note that it is the "reward" that is the same, not the individual blessings that we may receive. That reward is eternal life, but the blessings vary according to God's wisdom and will.

Many are called, few are chosen	Throughout the history of the covenant people, many of God's children have been invited to join the work but many of them reject that call. Others accept the call, but some find the work too hard, too long, the days too hot. Only those who endure to the end receive the full rewards.
The first shall be last, etc.	The Savior doesn't elaborate on what this means. It could suggest that the order in which we are called to the work doesn't determine in what order we shall be called home or how long we are asked to labor. But it could also imply that the blessings are the same for all, no matter when they were brought in, or something else that the Lord chose not to explain.

Here are some things to consider in what appears to be an inequitable treatment of the various workers in the vineyard.

- Paying each worker a penny. This can be misleading to us because a "penny" in our time is a pittance. The word translated as "penny" in the New Testament was the Roman *denarius*, the standard pay for one day's work. In our current monetary system where we pay such day laborers about $15 per hour, a twelve-hour day would bring $180, a worthwhile amount for a working man. That was what the foreman promised those he first hired. When he hired others later in the day, he promised that he would be fair with them but didn't cite a price. So, when it came time for a settlement, those who came later, especially the ones who had worked only one hour, were amazed when they received a full day's wage for one hour of labor.

- It is interesting that the foreman chose to pay the last laborers first, while the others stood by and watched. If he had started the other way around, the first ones hired would likely have left by the time he paid the last ones, and they would not have known what had happened and therefore would have had no reason to complain. However, one point of the parable is that the rewards that come from God for faithful service in His kingdom may differ, and sometimes not in what seems to us like a perfectly equitable way.

- The foreman's answer to those first disgruntled laborers was correct. They were not cheated in any way. He had kept his word. He had given them what he'd promised. Remember, each worker was not hired by the hour, but by the day, however long that day was. If they had finished their work in six hours instead of twelve, the foreman was obligated to give them the full amount.

- Nor were the ones who came later in the day lazy or slothful. They just hadn't been hired earlier. The early workers saw this as unfair and complained that they had been cheated. But they were not. Their irritation came not from getting less than promised, but from *their expectations of getting more!*

APPLICATION

So why would the Lord share this parable with His disciples, and especially the Twelve? Perhaps because they were themselves among those who were "the first" to be called to the work in the early morning of that new dispensation. Their service would be long and demanding. They would leave their wives and families sometimes for years at a time. There was no modern transportation or four-star hotels. And those early Apostles would be martyred in horrific ways.[3] According to traditions that stem from the earliest of those times, here is how some of the early Church leaders died:

Peter: crucified (upside down at his request)
Andrew: crucified
James: killed by the sword
Stephen: stoned to death
Philip: beheaded
Bartholomew: flayed alive
Thomas: killed with a spear
Matthew: burned alive or beheaded
James, son of Alphaeus: clubbed to death
Jude: killed with an axe
Matthias: beheaded
Paul: beheaded

This says nothing of the tens of thousands of Christians who were killed in the reign of the Roman emperors. Or the terrible persecutions the wicked have inflicted on the Lord's servants from the earliest of times down to our own day.

When we consider that most, if not all, of these Apostles were there when Jesus gave this parable, there is a subtle irony in what He taught them. The young man came asking how he could be chosen for the kingdom of God, but when he heard what was required, he turned away. And with that turning—unless at some later time he repented and gave up his riches—he chose not to be chosen for the very thing he so desired.

Then the Savior warned the Twelve and many other faithful disciples that the cost for their faithfulness might turn out to be very different from one another. Here is a dramatic example of how those "hours of labor" would differ found in the lives of the first Twelve

Apostles. In Acts 12, Luke records that not long after the death of Christ, King Herod turned against the early Christians and began to vigorously persecute them. James, the brother of John, who had only been an Apostle for a little more than three years, was put to the sword. He was the first apostolic martyr of that dispensation.

Peter too was caught up in Herod's wrath. But for some reason, Herod only had him put in prison, even though Peter was the senior Apostle at that time (see Acts 12:1–3). Peter was miraculously freed from prison and went on to lead the Church for several more decades. Early Christian historians report that Peter was later crucified in Rome during the persecutions of the Christians. Origen, an early Christian writer, says that Peter asked to be crucified upside down because he didn't feel worthy to suffer the same way that Jesus had died (see *Unger's Bible Dictionary*, 850).

But John, the brother of James, asked the resurrected Christ if he might stay on the earth to continue the Savior's work until Christ came again. The Savior granted him that privilege, and he is still out "laboring in the field" about 2,000 years later (see John 21:20–23; D&C 7:1–8). Compare that to James's few years and to Peter's decades. Could their sacrifices give us a more dramatic example of how the laborers in the Lord's vineyard are asked to labor for whatever time the Lord has need of them?

One possible lesson for us is clear. We should be grateful for any opportunity to labor in the work of the kingdom of God, wherever and whenever God sees fit to use us, and for as long as He wants us there. But in all cases, those who are determined to serve the Master well shall be richly rewarded for their faithful service.

Compare that to our day and our service in the kingdom. By any normal measure, we can see there is much inequity in the service of the Lord. Inequity yes, but not unfairness. Here are just a few examples of these "inequities" that come as a natural part of being called to work in the kingdom of God.

In our day, Joseph and Hyrum Smith were killed by a mob, and Parley P. Pratt was killed later while serving another mission. Since that time, no member of the Twelve has suffered martyrdom in our dispensation.

In the beginnings of the Church, many of the early converts were the first to be called to Jackson County, Missouri, to establish Zion. These were eventually driven by mobs out of the state of Missouri after men, women, and children suffered severe persecution or died because of the hardships and suffering they endured. We haven't seen that level of hatred and persecution against the Church in general since that time.

After many years of enduring that persecution, the pioneer Saints traveled 1,200 miles to find a place to worship safely. The average journey was three months. In our day, I walk to my chapel in five minutes.

As part of our elders quorum, I currently minister to two families. Both are within two blocks of my house. A friend of mine back east has been assigned five families who are scattered across a ward that is sixty miles long and forty miles wide.

Some missionaries are called to serve in places where many people are ready to receive the gospel. Others serve where very few are ready to receive their message. Some missionaries tract in areas where winter temperatures are far below zero. Others labor in areas where they have never seen snow.

Adam and Eve waited 4,000 years in the spirit world to be resurrected (see D&C 138:38–39). The faithful who die in this dispensation will have a much shorter time in the spirit world (see D&C 88:97–98).

A typical member of a stake presidency serves up to thirty hours per week for about nine years. Some of our callings in our stakes, wards, and branches take less than an hour a month. Yet, the "salary" is the same for both.

Here was an experience that seems to have particular relevance to what Jesus taught in this parable of laboring in the vineyard. I had lived in my ward for some time and knew most of the men in our priesthood quorum well. But we had an older couple who had joined the Church about six or seven months earlier and became ward members. They were very humble and eager to serve.

One Sunday, the elders quorum president said that they had some quorum business to conduct before the lesson. He announced that our quorum secretary was moving out of the ward and had to be released. He thanked him for his service, then presented the name of this new convert to be the new secretary. When he called for the sustaining vote, many hands came up. But when he asked for any who opposed that recommendation, one man near the back raised his hand.

That doesn't happen very often, and being a little bit flustered, the quorum president did something that he should not have done. He publicly asked the man why he objected.

His answer went something like this:

"I have nothing against this member of our quorum and can give you no reason why he shouldn't serve. But it's not fair. We've heard his story. He admits that he was in the merchant marines for twenty years and has been all around the world. He's told us that while he was single, he partook of all the 'goods' and 'entertainment' those ports around the world had to offer—drink, drugs, etc.

"I've been in this quorum for ten years or more. I don't drink or smoke. I serve where I'm called. I've been faithful to my wife for nearly forty years of marriage. And currently I have no Church calling. But he's the one you call to be the secretary to the quorum. Well, I object. It's not fair."

He finished by saying that he withdrew his vote of opposition. He had just wanted to be heard.

By the standards of the world, this effort we call "the work of the Lord" is not always fair. In the Church, we strive to eliminate injustice, but few of us expect perfect equity. Wouldn't that require the same number of hours for each calling? The same number of people we teach or minister to? The same length of service in our callings? The same level of challenges that different assignments require? The same hardships and dangers, or lack of them, in every calling?

And while we're talking inequity. Let us consider the Savior, the only person in all of human history who lived a perfect life and never violated a single commandment nor ever went contrary to the will of His Father. Yet He suffered for every sin and transgression ever committed. And not only that. He also atoned for the other disparities of this world—the sick versus the healthy, the poor versus the wealthy, the just versus the unjust, those born into stable, healthy lives versus those born into poverty or dysfunctional homes or who suffer from chronic illness or permanent disabilities. Through that infinite Atonement of Jesus Christ, all who are faithful receive the same reward, no matter how long or how short or how difficult their time in the vineyard turns out to be. Isn't this what the Savior meant when He said, "Learn that he who doeth the works of righteousness shall receive his reward, even peace in this world, and eternal life in the world to come" (D&C 59:23)?

I shall close with some insight about this concept given by those who, like Peter, James, and John, carry the apostolic assignment in the vineyard. President Dallin H. Oaks, while serving as a member of the Twelve, made reference to the parable of the laborers in the vineyard.

Many who come in the eleventh hour have been refined and prepared by the Lord in ways other than formal employment in the vineyard. . . . Similarly, the power of the Atonement and the principle of repentance show that we should never give up on loved ones who now seem to be making many wrong choices. Instead of being judgmental about others, we should be concerned about ourselves. We must not give up hope. We must not stop striving. We are children of God, and it is possible for us to become what our Heavenly Father would have us become. ("The Challenge to Become," *Ensign*, November 2000)

Elder Jeffrey R. Holland of the Quorum of the Twelve Apostles also spoke about this parable in general conference. He gave many wonderful insights and applications that we can draw from this parable. He spoke specifically of the "grumbling of the first laborers" when those who came later received the same amount of pay as they did. Then he admonished us with this counsel:

Brothers and sisters, there are going to be times in our lives when someone else gets an unexpected blessing or receives some special recognition. May I plead with us not to be hurt—and certainly not to feel envious—when good fortune comes to another person? We are not diminished when someone else is added upon. We are not in a race against each other to see who is the wealthiest or the most talented or the most beautiful or even the most blessed. . . . My beloved brothers and sisters, what happened in this story at 9:00 or noon or 3:00 is swept up in the grandeur of the universally generous payment at the end of the day. The formula of faith is to hold on, work on, see it through, and let the distress of earlier hours—real or imagined—fall away in the abundance of the final reward. Don't dwell on old issues or grievances—not toward yourself nor your neighbor nor even, I might add, toward this true and living Church. The majesty of your life, of your neighbor's life, and of the gospel of Jesus Christ will be made manifest at the last day, even if such majesty is not always recognized by everyone in the early going. So don't hyperventilate about something that happened at 9:00 in the morning when the grace of God is trying to reward you at 6:00 in the evening—whatever your labor arrangements have been through the day. ("The Laborers in the Vineyard," *Ensign*, May 2012)

NOTES

1. *Disciples* as used here means "follower." These could have been the Twelve specifically or others who believed in Him, or both.
2. The Resurrection.
3. We know that John the Beloved was translated and did not suffer death, but some early records indicate that the Romans put John in a vat of boiling oil but he was somehow protected and survived it because he had been promised to live until Christ returned.

Chapter 2

The
Rich Fool

CONTEXT AND SETTING

Jesus was teaching a large multitude one day when a man in the crowd interrupted Him. He asked Jesus to intervene with his brother and tell him to divide their father's inheritance with him.[1] The Savior's answer was short and to the point: "Who made me a judge or a divider over you?" Jesus then turned back to the multitude and said unto them: "Take heed, and beware of covetousness: for a man's life consists not in the abundance of the things which he possesseth" (Luke 12:13–15).

That answer suggests two things: First, that Jesus recognized that He had no legal standing in this personal family matter. Second, His ministry was about far more important things than using His influence to settle a family squabble over money.

After that brief interchange, Jesus immediately shared a short parable with those there.

THE PARABLE

And he spake a parable unto them, saying, The ground of a certain rich man brought forth plentifully: And he thought within himself, saying, What shall I do, because I have no room where to bestow my fruits?

And he said, This will I do: I will pull down my barns, and build greater; and there will I bestow all my fruits and my goods. And I will say to my soul, Soul, thou hast much goods laid up for many years; take thine ease, eat, drink, and be merry.

But God said unto him, Thou fool, this night thy soul shall be required of thee: then whose shall those things be, which thou hast provided?

So is he that layeth up treasure for himself, and is not rich toward God. (Luke 12:16–21)

ANALYSIS

The rich man was deeply pleased that he was prepared for a comfortable life for many years to come. Assuming that much of this wealth had come from the man's own effort and shrewdness, it's likely that he could have been a good manager and a hard worker and those traits had obviously paid off richly for him.

And yet, God called him a fool. Why? Because in all of that careful planning and preparation, he had given no thought to the fact that sooner or later he was going to die. The implication is that he was not considering how to prepare for the next stage of life that sooner or later comes to all of us. It is interesting that Jesus condemned his foolishness but did not suggest he was doing anything morally wrong. That is an important point for all of us. We can be foolish without being wicked. Remember the warning Jesus gave to this other son who was angry with his brother: "Beware of covetousness: for a man's life consisteth not in the abundance of the things which he possesseth" (Luke 12:15).

Was this the farmer's problem? Defining his life by his possessions? Is this why Jesus called him covetous and a fool? Why a fool? The description of the farmer shows intelligence, shrewdness, dedication, and wisdom. Hardly what we normally associate with being foolish. But Jesus said clearly that he was foolish because his primary focus was on his *temporal possessions*.

APPLICATION

In our day and time we have what we call "estate planning" or "preparing for retirement." Even though we know that there is a chance that we may die before we reach retirement age, those who are wise begin planning for that day decades in advance. They take a small portion of their income and put it away for the future. And this is a wise thing to do because the future always has some degree of uncertainty. So we are willing to set aside a portion of our salary now with an eye to the benefits that will bring in the future. Very few people would say that was a foolish use of our resources, even though we don't know for sure what is coming or, equally important, *when* it is coming.

But the parable is talking about another kind of estate planning—that time when death calls us home. There are many who don't believe in life after death, and so it is not surprising that they are not concerned about planning for a future life. But even so, many of them make preparations for a comfortable future. But in the time of Jesus, a majority of people believed that we continue to live after we die. So wisdom would clearly suggest that it is good to be a good steward in this life, but wise to also prepare for the life to come.

Sadly, while most people accept that reality, they go through this life as if it were the total sum of our existence. This was true of the farmer in the parable and the younger brother who was angry with his brother. Both were focused only on the "now." That is why they were both "fools."

Luke does not say whether the brother left in a huff after Jesus rebuked him or if he stayed to listen. But what is clear is that Jesus knew that the brother was not the only one listening to Him at that point. A word that the Gospel writers often use to describe who came to hear Jesus is *multitudes*. And surely Jesus was well aware that His words were being recorded and would be sent out to future generations, including our own. Shouldn't His admonition about being a fool in terms of our priority be a warning to us today? That is especially true of those who claim to be His disciples. We accept the reality of life after this life. We believe that how we live profoundly influences what that afterlife will be like. We know that no matter how large and how lavish our homes and barns are, we are not taking them with us into the spirit world and to the last Judgment.

With that in mind, shouldn't we all ask ourselves when we listen to His words if we too are not being a fool like the farmer and the angry brother? Wasn't Jesus speaking to all of us when He said, "So is he that layeth up treasure for himself, and is not rich toward God" (Luke 12:21).

And when that time comes for each of us, how many of us will fervently wish we had paid more attention to preparing for the next life than brooding about why life was not treating us more fairly? How many of us will wince when we hear those words, "Thou fool!" Or how many of us will learn the lesson of this parable and include that future life in our plans?

There is an old Arabic proverb that says:

> *Four things come not back:*
> *The spoken word;*
> *The sped arrow;*
> *The past life;*
> *The neglected opportunity.*

The parable of the rich fool isn't just a warning for the rich and the powerful. And the lesson of the rich fool is *not* just about earthly riches. Jesus was trying to teach us about focusing on the things that matter most, what we could divide into the spiritual and the temporal aspects of our lives.

It is of interest that while Jesus tells us what the rich farmer did to prepare for this life, He didn't specify what things he could have done to prepare spiritually. In a way, all of His teachings do that. In fact, we could sum up all of those possibilities in one simple phrase: "Faithfully live the gospel of Jesus Christ." And that would certainly be true. But there are other aspects of wise preparation in addition to gospel principles.

Keith B. McMullin, former Presiding Bishop of The Church of Jesus Christ of Latter-day Saints, shared an important insight in a short essay he called "Ambition versus Hard Work." Though he doesn't mention the parable, it appears from his choice of words that he may have had it in mind. Here are some excerpts from that essay:

> A young man, full of ambition and energy, enrolled in a fine university. . . . His goal was lofty—he wanted to become a doctor. His aim was ambitious—he wanted to be rich. He wanted to play football, so he sought out the coaches and eventually made the team. Now he could have the recognitions and bragging rights unique in the world of university sports. Such were the notions in his head.
>
> But he had given little thought to something that would ultimately dismantle his lofty and vain ambitions—he had failed to lay up in store. He had overlooked the importance of adequate preparation, the requirements of regular attendance and disciplined study. . . . The consequences were swift and merciless. . . .
>
> The day he found his 5-foot-8-inch, 170-pound body on the line of scrimmage opposite a mammoth lineman, he knew he was in the wrong sport. . . . [When he returned to

the classroom] unaccustomed to rigorous study, his eyes and mind refused to function after a brief time in the books.

The capstone of defeat was the final chemistry exam. His random answers to multiple-choice questions did not even approximate the law of averages. He failed miserably.

Hard work, a mission that awakened in him a correct vision of life's purposes, and unrelenting preparation eventually overcame the consequence of this brief period of foolishness.

Bishop McMullin then closed his essay with these words: "Even today, however, I still have nightmares about that chemistry class" ("Lay Up in Store," *Ensign*, May 2007).

President Boyd K. Packer, of the Quorum of the Twelve, reminded us of this reality with a short but terse observation: "There are many who struggle and climb and finally reach the top of the ladder, only to find that it is leaning against the wrong wall" (*That All May Be Edified*, 275).

The parable of the rich fool is a good example of why the subtitle of this book mentions mirrors and windows: When we hold up this parable as if it were a mirror, we are challenged to ask ourselves how we are doing in our own preparation for the life to come. But looking past that question, we can ask what might be the deeper and broader implications of the story. And that becomes a window through which we gain some eternal perspectives. We could belabor that point, but in the simplicity of the parable, we find enough complexity to occupy our thoughts for some time.

NOTES

1. In those times it was common for the eldest son to receive all of the estate, or the largest share of it. Sometimes, this didn't happen until after the father's death. But sometimes it was given, or a portion of it was given, when the father reached what we would call his retirement years. Other sons were sometimes given a portion of the inheritance. Sometimes this came directly from the father, but more often, the eldest son received it all, with the expectation—but not necessarily an obligation—to share with the others, too.

Chapter 3

The
Unprofitable Servant

CONTEXT AND SETTING

As we study the parables of Jesus, we quickly see that they vary in length and in the amount of detail included. Some take up much of a chapter. Others are only a brief paragraph. As we have seen, sometimes the Lord expounds on the parable at some length. In others, He gives no further explanation of why He chose to share that parable with us or the lesson it was meant to teach.

Often He spoke in parables to large multitudes. Other times His parables came in more private times with His closest disciples. In those cases, His purpose seems to have been to tutor them and help prepare them for that time when He would no longer be with them. Jesus was always teaching all of His followers what true discipleship meant and how to more consistently live the principles of the gospel. This is one reason why they are so valuable to us. They are every bit as applicable in the lives of modern believers as they were at the time Jesus taught them.

The parable that we are going to examine now comes as part of Luke's gospel, in a section where Jesus shared one parable after another. We can safely say that His disciples, and the Twelve especially, often felt overwhelmed and inadequate when He was teaching them.

On this day, Jesus began teaching His disciples[1] about offenses—or what we today would call sins and transgressions that especially harm others—and the consequences that come with them. He admonished His listeners to forgive them "that trespass against thee," even seven times if necessary (see Luke 17:1–4).

Luke reports that the Apostles then asked: "Lord, Increase our faith" (Luke 17:5). This seems to be a plea for deeper understanding of what He had just taught them. If they were to exercise faith enough to forgive as He had just taught them, they felt like they needed much more faith than what they were feeling at that time.

Jesus began by teaching them about the principle of faith, which probably discouraged them even further, for He drew on two metaphors from the plant world common to the Holy Land. "And the Lord said, If ye had faith as a grain of mustard seed, ye might say unto this sycamine tree, Be thou plucked up by the root, and be thou planted in the sea; and it should obey you" (Luke 17:6). Understanding a little more of the nature of these two plants adds depth to our understanding of the parables.

First, the mustard seed. The mustard seed was one of the smallest of seeds found in the botanical world. A single seed can grow to a healthy bush. A small handful of these tiny seeds sown together will eventually grow into a large thicket of bushes with many branches covered with bright yellow flowers. The contrast between the size of the seed and the size of the plant dramatically suggested how great things could come from small beginnings.

Some readers of the Bible assume that the sycamine tree is an alternate spelling of the sycamore tree, which is native to North America. But the sycamine tree is not part of that family, but is related to the mulberry tree, which was common in the Middle East. What makes this analogy so powerful is that the sycamine is a tree that grows to a height of about thirty feet, with wide, spreading branches and a trunk that can be two or more feet in diameter.

However, because of the hot, dry weather common to the Middle East, the sycamine's root system goes deep into the earth. To pull up a full-grown sycamine tree is nearly impossible, even if one digs all around it. The roots are so strong and so deep that even if the tree is cut off at ground level, the roots can survive and start a new tree. For Jesus to say that a person with faith no larger than a mustard seed had the power to "pluck up" a sycamine tree would have been impressive indeed. Immediately following that analogy, the Savior launched into the parable.

THE PARABLE

But which of you, having a servant plowing or feeding cattle, will say unto him by and by, when he is come from the field, Go and sit down to meat? And will not rather say unto him, Make ready wherewith I may sup, and gird thyself, and serve me, till I have eaten and drunken; and afterward thou shalt eat and drink?

Doth he thank that servant because he did the things that were commanded him? I trow[2] not.

So likewise ye, when ye shall have done all those things which are commanded you, say, We are unprofitable servants: we have done that which was our duty to do. (Luke 17:7–10)

ANALYSIS

One thing to note about this parable is that it was directly tied to Jesus's reference to the mustard seed and the power of faith. That reference seemed to provide context but without specifying how it was related. Another is that Luke did not give us any further explanation of why Jesus felt this was something they needed to know. However, what immediately preceded this parable—the analogy of the mustard seed—suggests that it was also about strengthening our faith and understanding of the gospel.

There is something else to remember at this point. The disciples—and especially the Twelve—were ordinary people who chose to accept, believe, and then follow the Savior. But Jesus, though mortal, was perfect in every respect. And that meant that He was a perfect Teacher! In His infinite wisdom, He chose to teach His followers many profound spiritual truths. And He often did that by drawing on everyday things all around them. Sometimes He elaborated on what He said. Other times no more is recorded. And the Gospel writers make it clear that many times, Jesus left His listeners wondering what He was trying to teach them.

Here again we have a parable that, in some ways, seems troubling at first. As written in the King James Version, it suggests that the master of the house is somewhat heartless and acts selfishly toward his servants. The very word "unprofitable" used here suggests that the servant provided no benefit to the master's household. But common sense would suggest that if that were true, the servant would have been terminated long before this point.

Adam Clarke, a renowned Bible scholar in the early 1800s, commented on why the master in the parable did what he did:

> It is never supposed that the master waits on the servant—the servant is bound to wait on his master, and to do every thing for him to the uttermost of his power: nor does the former expect *thanks* for it, for he is *bound* by agreement to act thus, because of the stipulated reward, which is considered to be equal to *all the service* he can perform. (*Clarke's Commentary*, 5:467)

In the Phillips Modern English translation of the New Testament, the wording makes it clear that the servant is valued and that the point the Savior is trying to make is more about our relationship to God than the relationship between the servant and his master.

> If any of you have a servant plowing or looking after the sheep, are you likely to say to him when he comes in from the fields, "Come straight in and sit down to your meal"? Aren't you more likely to say, "Get my supper ready: change your coat and wait while I eat and drink: and then, when I've finished, you can have your meal"? Do you feel particularly grateful to your servant for doing what you tell him? I don't think so. It is the same with yourselves[3]—when you have done everything that you are told to do, you can say, "We are not good as servants, for we have only done what we ought to do." (Phillips, Luke 17:7–10)

With that clarification in mind, let us again set up the parabolic in the structure used earlier, which can help us better understand what Jesus was trying to teach us.

The servant	The servant here seems to represent any or all of God's children, but especially those who are laboring in the kingdom of God.
The master of the household	Ultimately, that would be God the Father and His Son Jesus Christ. But it could include leaders in the kingdom who also lead out in the work.
The master serving the servant	This is not the proper order of things in human relations. The servant is hired to serve his master. Since God has already offered each of

His children infinite blessings, even if we serve Him faithfully all of our lives, it can't begin to equal what we owe Him. There is no indication that the master mistreated the servant, but simply that he expected him to continue doing his duties when he came in from the field.

The master's role   The master (whether male or female) has the responsibility to care for the family, maintain a good living for them, and help the family meet all of their needs.

The servant's role   It simply is to help the master meet obligations, i.e., carry out the work required to keep the family safe, healthy, and happy. In our roles as servants in the household of God we are expected to accept His plan and His will, not create our own or try to counsel God in how to do His work. In the kingdom, that would include sharing the gospel and serving and ministering to others.

APPLICATION

The Savior has told us throughout the scriptures what the "wages and benefits" are that come to us when we faithfully serve our Master. Here are just three examples. There are dozens of others.

- "Learn of me, and listen to my words; walk in the meekness of my Spirit, and you shall have peace in me" (D&C 19:23).
- "He that doeth the works of righteousness shall receive his reward, even peace in this world, and eternal life in the world to come" (D&C 59:23).

- "Come unto me, all ye that labour and are heavy laden, and I will give you rest. Take my yoke upon you, and learn of me; for I am meek and lowly in heart: and ye shall find rest unto your souls. For my yoke is easy, and my burden is light" (Matthew 11:28–30).

We could list many others, such as temple blessings, the joy and growth that comes with missionary service, the blessings of happy and faithful families, and more.

When we ponder this concept carefully, it becomes clear that the covenant the Father and the Son have made with us is so rich in blessings, so broad in its benefits, and so infinite in its joy that no matter how much we serve Them or how much good we do in this world, we cannot begin to repay Them for all that we owe to Them.

We have to be very careful in this servant/master relationship that we don't forget that the Master has already provided us the food, shelter, care, and everything else that we have in this life. So to start to assume that God somehow owes us blessings and rewards and should be there to serve our needs is a subtle form of pride.

When we consider those aspects of the parable, we can better see the point that Jesus was making. Even if we were to serve God every moment of our lives, giving Him full service even into eternity, that cannot begin to repay the infinite and marvelous blessings that come from Him. A perfect, total, and utterly dedicated life of service to Him and His work cannot put Him in our debt, because what we receive from Him is infinitely more. And we have not *added one thing to His perfection that would enrich Him*, that is, that would add to His perfection. Therefore, we are now and always will be forever in His debt. We are now and always will be forever unprofitable servants.

And yet, sometimes in our myopic pride and arrogance we feel that our acts of obedience somehow put God in our debt. That He owes us His thanks for us doing so well. A Christian minister likened this prideful attitude to assuming that God is our personal vending machine. We earn our quarters by being good, serving in the kingdom, helping others, etc.

Then when some crisis comes up in our lives, we put a quarter into the vending machine, then stand back and wait for the blessings to pop out and fulfill our needs. And if they don't, some of us actually grow angry because He is not giving us what we think He owes us. And in our pride and haughtiness, sometimes we say, "All right, then. If God won't answer my prayers, I'll show Him. I'll stop praying to Him. I'll quit going to church. That will show Him."

Some time ago, a close friend shared an experience that he'd had in his own personal quest to better serve the Lord. He held this parable up as if it were a mirror and sought to better understand it. In doing so, he provided a powerful reminder of the principle taught in this parable. These are his words:

> One morning in my scripture studies, I was reflecting on my life, thinking of the numerous times Heavenly Father had blessed me and my family. Many were simple blessings. Many were quite profound, some even astounding. As I pondered on that, there came a deep sense of gratitude, and as I knelt down to pray, and I thought to myself: "How can I ever repay Him for all of that He has blessed me with?"
>
> To my great surprise, the parable of the unprofitable servant came into my mind. I had wondered before why the Savior had given this particular parable, but at this point I wasn't sure what that had to do with my life.
>
> So I shrugged off the thought and went on with my prayer. I prayed: "Heavenly Father, show me how I can repay Thee in some small way for all of the many blessings Thou hast given to me and to my family."

Even as I said that, there came a simple thought, but it came with great clarity: "The word 'repay' means to 'give back full value for something received.' And that is not possible in this case. There is no way you can even begin to pay back the Father and the Son for what They have done for you and others."

I was quite taken aback by that thought. Then I began to understand. First of all, God's blessings are far beyond anything of worldly value I have. Second, His blessings are infinite in number and in value. How do you pay back a debt like that? Third, He is God—that means that He is perfect in every way—His power, glory, knowledge, love, and every other attribute is without flaw. What does He need from me that could ever possibly benefit Him? Absolutely nothing!

And yet He rejoices in our desire to express our thanks to Him. But that doesn't change the reality that there is nothing I can give to Them which would even begin to repay the debt.

It was a stunning thought, but I instantly knew it was a profound truth. As I pondered on that, I came to this conclusion: "It is not possible for the finite to repay the Infinite. Not ever!"

It was a wonderful learning moment, but I felt a deep sadness because I so wanted to do something in return for all that I had received.

Then came this follow-up thought: "While you cannot repay Them—not ever!—you can express your gratitude for those blessings. And you can show your thanks not just in words, but in deeds and action."

I was astounded. "Of course!" I thought. "It is so

simple. When we serve others, we serve *Them*! And They are deeply grateful for that and will joyfully bless us even more."

Another question quickly followed: "But how? I have a ministering assignment, and I'll strive to take that much more seriously than I have before, but I want to do more than that. I want to *do* what matters to Them." And once again immediately there came into my mind the answer.

"Peter said that Jesus 'went about doing good' (Acts 10:38). So there is your model. Jesus is your Exemplar. He is your perfect Mentor. Follow His example. How? It's simple. Serve! Love! Minister! Lift! Lighten! Cheer! Bless! Comfort! Do that and your desire will be filled and the Father and the Son will accept your efforts."

That's been about three years ago now. Every day in my prayers, I ask my Father in Heaven for opportunities to express my gratitude to Him and to His Son through serving others and doing good, by striving harder to *be* better, to *do* better, and to *serve* better. And He has answered those prayers again and again. Usually they come as small, simple things. A smile. A kind word. A note left anonymously in the mailbox.

When I say my prayers have been answered, I'm not talking about great miracles here. But they are things that make a significant difference in people's lives. And each Sunday in sacrament meeting, I try to remember to really, truly renew my covenant that I will "always remember Him."

President Russell M. Nelson has spoken of the joys that come from reaching out and helping others. Though he doesn't mention the parable of the unprofitable servant, he emphasizes that principle taught therein:

One of life's sweetest returns is the privilege of rendering significant service of worth to others. To be able to do for fellow human beings something they could not do for themselves brings matchless satisfaction. Years of preparation are worth it. Joy is derived in Church service. Alma so expressed this thought: "That perhaps I may be an instrument in the hands of God to bring some soul to repentance . . . is my joy" (Alma 29:9). (*Teachings of Russell M. Nelson*, 358)

We are all—even the very best of us—unprofitable servants. This simple parable reminds us of that, especially as we hold it up as a mirror to our souls and a window to eternity. We close with the wonderful words of King Benjamin, who understood this principle very clearly:

If I, whom ye call your king, who has spent his days in your service, and yet has been in the service of God, do merit any thanks from you, O how you ought to thank your heavenly King! I say unto you, my brethren, that if you should render all the thanks and praise which your whole soul has power to possess, to that God who has created you, and has kept and preserved you, and has caused that ye should rejoice, and has granted that ye should live in peace one with another—I say unto you that if ye should serve him who has created you from the beginning, and is preserving you from day to day, by lending you breath, that ye may live and move and do according to your own will, and even supporting you from one moment to another—I say, if ye should serve him with all your whole souls yet ye would be unprofitable servants. And behold, all that he requires of you is to keep his commandments. . . . Therefore, if ye do keep his commandments he doth bless you and prosper you.

. . . And secondly, he doth require that ye should do as he hath commanded you; for which if ye do, he doth immediately bless you; and therefore he hath paid you. And ye are still indebted unto him, and are, and will be, forever and ever; therefore, of what have ye to boast? (Mosiah 2:19–24)

NOTES

1. *Apostle* is an office in the Melchizedek Priesthood, and a title given to those who hold that office. The word *disciple* as used in the New Testament is a more generic term coming from the Greek word meaning a learner, pupil, or follower, which would also include the Apostles (see *Strong's Concordance*, 3101).

2. Trow: to think, suppose, or judge (see *Strong's Concordance*, 1380).

3. "Yourselves" and "you" as used here may suggest that Jesus was speaking to the apostles, not to the multitude at this point.

Chapter 4

The Sower
and the Soils

CONTEXT AND SETTING

In this section of our study, we are examining parables that focus on what it means to live as covenant disciples so that we can develop a positive relationship with our Father in Heaven, His Son, Jesus Christ, and the Holy Ghost. To put it into a phrase that we often hear today, these parables show us how to better *get on* and then *stay on* the covenant path that leads to salvation and exaltation. That is our ultimate goal because only in that way can we receive a fullness of joy.

Fortunately, Jesus often taught about true discipleship. Again and again in His teachings, and especially in the parables, we find practical, down-to-earth counsel on how to change our hearts so they become more open to the promptings and guidance of the Spirit. Without the influence of the Spirit, there is no other way that we can find our way back to the presence of the Father. So these teachings become practical guides on how to incorporate gospel principles and actually apply them in our lives.

According to Matthew, this was the first parable Jesus taught. All three of the synoptic Gospel writers—Matthew, Mark, and Luke—include this parable in their Gospel. Matthew's account of this parable has a few more details and a few significant differences from the accounts of Mark and Luke, so we shall use his for our study.

In all three accounts (Matthew 13:3–23; Mark 4:2–20; Luke 8:4–15), there is no specific event mentioned that brought forth this parable. Jesus was staying at Capernaum, a prosperous fishing village on the north shore of the Sea of Galilee. Matthew and Mark both record that He was at the seaside and a large throng of people had come to hear Him. The crowd was large enough that Jesus entered one of the fishing boats and moved a short distance away from the shore and began to teach them. Without any preamble, He began with this parable.

THE PARABLE

And he spake many things unto them in parables, saying, Behold, a sower went forth to sow;

And when he sowed, some seeds fell by the way side, and the fowls came and devoured them up:

Some fell upon stony places, where they had not much earth: and forthwith they sprung up, because they had no deepness of earth: And when the sun was up, they were scorched; and because they had no root, they withered away.

And some fell among thorns; and the thorns sprung up, and choked them:

But other fell into good ground, and brought forth fruit, some an hundredfold, some sixtyfold, some thirtyfold. Who hath ears to hear, let him hear. (Matthew 13:3–9)

This form of teaching evidently caught the disciples by surprise, for when an opportunity presented itself, they asked Him, "Why speakest thou unto them in parables?" (Matthew 13:10). That was most likely later in the day when they were alone with Him. And for that reason, the term *disciples* in this case suggests that this might have been only the Twelve. Jesus answered their question by explaining that people have different levels of spiritual readiness, and parables have a unique way of conveying different understanding to people with various levels of readiness. In some cases, their hearts are hardened against light and truth and they refuse to hear and understand. Jesus said this method allowed those who were spiritually ready to be taught, while those who were not ready would not be condemned by the knowledge (see Matthew 13:13–15).

Referencing a prophecy from Isaiah, Jesus said, "By hearing ye shall hear, and shall not understand; and seeing ye shall see, and shall not perceive: For this people's heart is waxed gross,[1] and their ears are dull of hearing, and their eyes they have closed" (Matthew 13:14–15). This suggests that an unwillingness to hear and understand may sometimes be a matter of choice, while in others it comes from a lack of understanding spiritual principles. In this instance, Jesus seemed to be saying that parables by their very design were meant to both *reveal* and *conceal* meaning, depending on the spiritual readiness of the listener. Jesus then said to them:

> But blessed are your eyes, for they see: and your ears, for they hear. For verily I say unto you, That many prophets and righteous men have desired to see those things which ye see, and have not seen them; and to hear those things which ye hear, and have not heard them. Hear ye therefore the parable of the sower. (Matthew 13:16–18)

And with that encouragement, Jesus then gave them some keys for interpreting the parable.

> When any one heareth the word of the kingdom, and understandeth it not, then cometh the wicked one, and catcheth away that which was sown in his heart. This is he which received seed by the way side.

But he that received the seed into stony places, the same is he that heareth the word, and anon[2] with joy receiveth it; Yet hath he not root in himself, but dureth for a while: for when tribulation or persecution ariseth because of the word, by and by he is offended.

He also that received seed among the thorns is he that heareth the word; and the care of this world, and the deceitfulness of riches, choke the word, and he becometh unfruitful.

But he that received seed into the good ground is he that heareth the word, and understandeth it; which also beareth fruit, and bringeth forth, some an hundredfold, some sixty, some thirty. (Matthew 13:19–23)

ANALYSIS

Before setting up our parallel structure for this parable, let us remember a few important points.

1. We are not talking about modern farming methods here. In that time, there were no tractors, there was no mechanized equipment to plow, harrow, plant, and harvest the seed. It was all done by human labor.

2. If the farmer was lucky, he might have a donkey or an ox to work the ground and prepare it for planting. In many cases the plowing was done by hand.

3. For the most part, these were small plots of land, probably no more than an acre or two, and sometimes less.

4. The seed here is likely wheat, which, as now, was a staple part of people's diets.

5. To sow the seed, the farmer used what is known as the "broadcast method." He carried a cloth bag filled with the seed, which was slung over one shoulder so that the pouch that held the grain rested

on the farmer's hip. He would then walk from one end of the field to the other, systematically taking handfuls of grain and flinging it sideways so as to scatter the seed evenly across the soil.

6. Most important, keep in mind that it is not the sower nor the seed that is the main focus of the parable. Rather it is the *nature of the soil itself.* Though some scholars call this the parable of the sower, it is the nature of the soil that determines the harvest, not the sower.

Here are some key elements of the parable and possible meanings for our personal lives.

The seed	The gospel, the good word of God, in all of its complexity and simplicity. Note that Jesus said, "When anyone heareth *the word of the kingdom*" (Matthew 13:19; emphasis added).
The sower	Though Jesus did not give a specific interpretation, it is clear that the sower represents Jesus Himself, and, by extension, anyone who serves faithfully in His kingdom spreading the word of Christ and His doctrine. These are the ones who "broadcast" the word to the world. And *broadcast* is a good description of how it is done. We teach everyone who will listen, knowing that in many cases the word will immediately be rejected. We use every method to do so. The most common way throughout time has been face-to-face contact, teaching one on one. Missionaries of all generations spend their time talking to people. Some ignore them. Some stone them. And some are touched in their hearts and accept the seed and it begins to grow. We also spread the seed

through meetings, conferences, worldwide broadcasts. We use print media, radio and television, the internet, billboards, and the mail.

The soils

The soils are the central focus of this parable. Jesus made it clear that the soils represent the "hearts" of men. Thus, the Lord describes four different conditions of people's hearts, which we shall explore further below.

Fowls of the air

In the Matthew account, the fowls are referred to as "the wicked one," suggesting Satan, and by extension, those who serve him. Some scholars believe Jesus was referring to what we call crows or ravens. Ravens are found all across the world and are common in the Middle East even today. By nature, ravens are raucous, aggressive, often bullying other birds and stealing their food. They eat carrion and other spoiled food, which suggests pollution and corruption.

The harvest

Ripe wheat is the desired end result of planting the seed. It seems to represent the time when our lives here on earth will end—when further growth in this life ends. The difference in yield is not because the seed—the word of God—is lacking in quality, but rather that the soil in which the seed is spread directly affects the yield. The different responses to the gospel primarily rest in the hearts of men, or the four kinds of soil. The primary differences in the

> amount of wheat harvested is not due to fault in the seed, but because the hearts of men vary widely and they respond differently to the word of God or they have differing levels of ability and gifts.

It is clear that understanding what each type of soil represents is the key to understanding the parable of the sower and the soils. So let us briefly examine the four types of soil more closely.

1. *The wayside.* In modern English, "wayside" suggests a pleasant place, with perhaps a bench to sit on with trees and shade. But that is misleading. The Greek word that is translated as "wayside" means a "traveled way," such as a trail, path, or roadway. There the soil is hard and impenetrable (see *Strong's Concordance*, 3598). *Pathway* or *walkway* would be another good word. The modern equivalent would be a gravel sidewalk.

In the Holy Land at this time, few farmers had fences or rock walls to separate their property from others. Their boundaries were typically marked out by the pathways between the farm properties. Remember, the wheat seed was scattered through the broadcast method, so it was only natural that some of the seed would fall on these strips of hard ground where the seed would never take root. We might say that this could be described as the "hardened heart."

2. *Stony places.* This wording can also be misleading, for it conjures up a place strewn with many rocks and even small boulders. But the Savior's description of how the seed responds to this "stony" ground suggests something quite different. In many areas of the world, including the Holy Land, there are places where underlying sheets of bedrock—often sandstone or limestone—are covered with shallow layers of sand or dirt. In some such places, that soil can be several feet deep, in others barely inches thick. This soil is a place

where seeds can sprout and grow in the spring rains. But that is deceiving, for in many places the soil is not deep enough to let the roots go down deep and find sufficient moisture to sustain them through the heat of summer. At first, the plants seem to thrive, but as the heat continues, they quickly shrivel up and die.

Matthew records the Savior as defining the "heat of the day" as being "tribulation or persecution" (Matthew 13:21). Mark designated it as "affliction or persecution [that] ariseth for the word's sake" (Mark 4:17). Luke states, "They on the rock are they, which, when they hear, receive the word with joy; and . . . in time of temptation fall away" (Luke 8:13). The point is that there are some people who gladly accept the gospel message, but once they are asked to commit themselves to living as the faithful do or are faced with difficult trials, their enthusiasm quickly dies. Their "roots" hit solid rock and they quickly return to their previous lives. We will characterize these hearts as "shallow hearts."

3. *Thorny ground.* Here, the problem is not that the soil is poor in quality. Just the opposite is true. Here the soil is rich and deep and can sustain the thick growth of plant life. In the Holy Land, such fields of thorns—we call them thistles in America—grow so thick that even a horse cannot push its way through them.

Here again the three Gospel writers describe the cause of this choking abundance as a "heart problem" but in slightly different language: Matthew likens the thorns to "the care of this world, and the deceitfulness of riches" (Matthew 13:22). Mark said it was "the cares of this world, and the deceitfulness of riches, and the lusts of other things entering in" that choked the word and led them to become "unfruitful" (Mark 4:19). Luke's description is similar, but he added new insights as to why they failed in their commitment: "And that which fell among thorns are they, which, when they have heard, go forth, and are choked with cares and riches and pleasures of this life; and bring no fruit to perfection" (Luke 8:14).

4. *Good ground.* This fourth and final type of soil differs in the nutrients that bring forth the wheat. Farmers understand this principle well and adapt to the nature of the soils as necessary. This last group is categorized as "good soils," but even they differ in richness and thus produce differing amounts of grain in the harvest.

Again it is instructive to see how the Gospel authors described this last group. Matthew states: "He that received seed into the good ground is he that heareth the word, and understandeth; which also beareth fruit" (Matthew 13:23). Mark's account is much the same as Matthew's. Luke says: "But that on the good ground are they, which in an honest and good heart, having heard the word, keep it, and bring forth fruit with patience" (Luke 8:15).

APPLICATION

Elder James E. Talmage, who served in the Quorum of the Twelve Apostles in the early 1900s and wrote a classic study of the life of Jesus that he named *Jesus the Christ*, made this observation about this particular parable:

> Even . . . as judged by the recognized standards of rhetorical construction and logical arrangement of its parts, *this parable holds first place among productions of its class.* Though commonly known to us as the Parable of the Sower, the story could be expressively designated as the Parable of the Four Kinds of Soil. *It is the ground upon which the seed is cast, to which the story most strongly directs our attention, and which so aptly is made to symbolize the softened or the hardened heart, the clean or the thorn-infested soil.* (*Jesus the Christ,* 284–85; emphasis added)

Once again I stress that the key to understanding the parable is in understanding the nature of the four soils—or the difference in the hearts—upon which the seed falls. All three Gospel writers stress that likeness to *men's hearts* (see Matthew 13:19; Mark 4:15; Luke 8:12).

We are not talking about the organ that keeps life going. We are speaking of the heart as it is used metaphorically throughout the scriptures to represent the inner person, the "real me" inside each of us. Because it is the heart that drives the blood through the body and keeps us alive and healthy by providing nutrients, protecting us from infections, and cleansing our bodies of impurities, the heart is a powerful symbol of our soul and nature. Note the many modifiers we use when we speak of the heart: broken hearts, happy hearts, cold hearts, warm hearts, hard hearts, soft hearts, hearts like stone, and some people who "have no heart at all."

It is interesting to note that in the four standard works, the word *heart* is found in some form or another about fifteen hundred times. Here is a very brief sampling of how it is used:

- "The foolish imaginations of his heart" (1 Nephi 2:11).
- I "did soften my heart" (1 Nephi 2:16).
- I "grieved because of the hardness of their hearts" (1 Nephi 2:18).[3]
- Men set their hearts upon riches (see Helaman 3:36) and on the things of the world (D&C 121:35).
- As he began his sermon, King Benjamin urged his people, "Open your ears that you may hear, and your hearts that you may understand" (Mosiah 2:9).
- Through works of darkness, Satan gets hold on the hearts of men (see Helaman 6:30).
- The Lord speaks to our hearts (see D&C 8:2).

- We are to love our spouses with all our hearts (see D&C 42:22).
- "I, the Lord, require the hearts of the children of men" (D&C 64:22).
- Jesus said of the leaders of the Jews, "O fools, and slow of heart to believe" (Luke 24:25).
- Before his martyrdom, Stephen called his persecutors "stiff-necked and uncircumcised in heart and ears" (Acts 7:51).
- The ten commandments direct us to "love the Lord thy God with all thine heart, and with all thy soul, and with all thy might" (Deuteronomy 6:5).

President Dallin H. Oaks wrote two books in which he used the word *heart* in the title: *The Pure in Heart* and *With Full Purpose of Heart*. In the preface of the first book, he wrote: "In the language of the scriptures, the word *heart* is a powerful figurative expression, rich in meaning. It is the primary instrument used to teach us that from the perspective of eternity and in terms of God's commandments the hidden thoughts of our minds are just as important as the observed actions of our bodies" (*The Pure in Heart*, viii).

In his book *To Draw Closer to God*, President Henry B. Eyring also spoke of the role of the heart in striving for spiritual growth and perfection:

> Now, the key in all of this is to have a soft heart. A soft heart has nothing to do with being a coward. In fact, the bravest people I've ever known have had the softest hearts. I've known of situations in which the Lord's servants have put their lives in jeopardy because of their love for God and his children. When people love enough, and their hearts are softened enough, there's nothing they wouldn't do in the service of the Lord Jesus Christ. . . . This is what the Savior

said about a soft heart: "And ye shall offer for a sacrifice unto me a broken heart and a contrite spirit. And whoso cometh unto me with a broken heart and a contrite spirit, him will I baptize with fire and with the Holy Ghost" (3 Nephi 9:20). (*To Draw Closer to God*, 109)

President Russell M. Nelson, who was a heart surgeon, drew an analogy between a heart that is physically damaged and those that have spiritual weaknesses:

> A surgeon can repair or replace a mitral valve that has lost its integrity. But no surgical procedure can be performed for loss of spiritual integrity of heart. Such breakdown is under the individual control. Isaiah observed that "thou . . . didst debase thyself" (Isaiah 57:9). The wise fisherman inspects his nets regularly. Should any flaw be detected, he repairs the defect, without delay. . . . Recorded revelation gives similar instruction. The Lord said, "Remember therefore from whence thou are fallen, and repent, and do the first works" (Revelation 2:5). So the wise assess personal cords of integrity on a daily basis. You are the one to repair it. Indeed, you have an obligation to do so. Words of Isaiah, though referencing service to others, apply equally to ourselves. He said: "Strengthen ye the weak hands, and confirm the feeble knees. Say to them that are of a fearful heart, Be strong" (Isaiah 35:3–4). (*Teachings*, 153)

In closing, here is a question that comes to mind as we apply this parable to real life. Why does the Lord only mention requiring the heart here? Why doesn't He also ask us for the head? Or the hands? Or the feet? There are places where He asks that we totally give all of ourselves to the work, but again and again, as seen in the sheer number of times the heart is mentioned, the scriptures teach us that the heart is the core of our being, the center of our spirituality. Or lack of it. Thus the heart represents the "inner me, the true me." With that in mind, is it any wonder that the very first of Christ's parables would focus on the nature of our hearts?

In the closing chapter of 2 Nephi, Nephi, son of Lehi, made this declaration: "For when a man speaketh by the power of the Holy Ghost the power of the Holy Ghost carrieth it *unto* the hearts of men" (2 Nephi 33:1; emphasis added).

Note that choice of words. "Unto," not "into." Is that just a typographical oversight in the translation? Is the Lord satisfied with just "unto" in this case?

Ponder on that for a moment. That simple choice of words teaches us a profound truth. We make decisions in our minds, but it is in the heart that we determine whether to pursue or abandon those decisions. Thus the heart is the center of our moral agency.

Our hearts are like a gate that swings open or shut, but only on our command. To put it another way, *we are the gatekeepers of our own hearts!* We are the ones who choose what we let in or keep out.

Elder David A. Bednar described this unique privilege that God has given to us: "A learner exercising agency by acting . . . opens his or her heart to the Holy Ghost and invites His teaching, testifying power, and confirming witness. . . . *Ultimately, thowever, he content of a message and the witness of the Holy Ghost penetrates into the heart only if a receiver allows them to enter*" (David A. Bednar, *Ensign*, Sept. 2007; emphasis added).

As we conclude our examination of this powerful parable that describes the various hearts that we create for ourselves, let us remember this simple—but profound!—summary from the Savior Himself:

"I, the Lord, require the hearts of the children of men" (D&C 64:22).

NOTES

1. Thick, fat, stupid (see *Strong's Concordance*, 4078).
2. Straight away, immediately.
3. In the first book of the Book of Mormon, Nephi uses the word *heart* forty-three times.

Part II

Gospel Application

Chapter 5

The
Unmerciful Servant

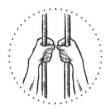

CONTEXT AND SETTING

In the first section we discussed parables that gave us insight into our relationship with Deity, including the Father, the Son, and the Holy Ghost. In this section we shall examine several parables that teach how to improve that relationship, strengthen our faith, and deepen our commitment to the Godhead that we serve by applying gospel principles more effectively in our lives. These principles are found throughout the four standards works, but several of the parables of Jesus give us some of those principles in a unique form. In this section of the book, we shall examine some of those parables in detail.

Though the writers of the four Gospels don't give a lot of detail on the sequence of various events in the mortal life of the Savior, it appears that at this point, Jesus was well along in His three-year ministry. The numbers flocking to hear Him and the numbers who chose to become His disciples seem to have increased almost daily. And the Twelve and the Seventy He had chosen to be leaders in the kingdom were clearly maturing in their understanding of the gospel as Jesus was with them almost every day. But even with that growing experience, one also gets the feeling that virtually every day with the

Savior was a new—and often humbling!—learning experience for them.

This parable is found in a chapter where Matthew recorded several events in quick sequence. It began with a question from His disciples about who would be the greatest in the kingdom of heaven. Whether this came from the Twelve or from other followers, Matthew doesn't say. But considering what the Twelve had given up to follow Him, it could have been something they were wondering about.

Whoever it was that asked the question, the Savior's reply likely came as surprise. He called a little child to Him and taught them that this was the model for anyone seeking to find a place in the kingdom of heaven. He expounded at some length on this theme (see Matthew 18:1–14).

Jesus had recently promised the Twelve that they would receive the keys of the kingdom so they could lead the Church after He was gone (see Matthew 16:13–20). After that experience, He took Peter, James, and John up on a mountain, where they had a very sacred experience when Jesus was transfigured before them and Moses and Elijah appeared to them. The voice of the Father also testified that Jesus was His most beloved Son (see Matthew 17:1–13).

All of that suggests that at this point in His ministry, Jesus was sensing an urgency to prepare them to take up the burden of leadership after He was gone. They were probably sensing that too, to some degree, and so the Twelve seemed eager to gain as much knowledge and experience from Him as they could.

Sometime after that experience, Peter came to Jesus with another question. Though it doesn't say this, it seems likely that Peter had been pondering on some previous teaching of the Savior. "Lord," he said, "how oft shall my brother[1] sin against me, and I forgive him? Till seven times?" (Matthew 18:21).

The Rabbis at that time stated that the Mosaic law required that when people were wronged by someone, they were obligated to forgive that person *three* times. If the offender didn't change after that, then the offended party was justified in taking action against him. For Peter to ask if seven times would be sufficient—more than double what was required by the Mosaic law!—suggests that he was eager to show he was learning and growing. With that in mind, the Savior's answer must have taken Peter aback.

Jesus said: "I say not unto thee, Until seven times: but, Until seventy times seven" (Matthew 18:22).

What? Forgive someone *four hundred and ninety times?* That is a staggering number. It seems almost incomprehensible that one offender could sin against another person that many times. Was Jesus actually suggesting that he keep count, or was this a deliberate exaggeration of the numbers to suggest to Peter that if you're keeping count, perhaps you don't understand the true spirit of forgiveness?

Some Bible scholars believe that the Savior chose hyperbole—a deliberate exaggeration—to make a point with His senior Apostle. Perhaps Jesus was suggesting something like this: If you are carefully counting the number of times you are wronged with the intent to strike back once you have fulfilled the requirement, then you have not understood the spirit of the gospel.

Matthew doesn't tell us how Peter responded to what he was taught. Immediately after his exchange with Peter, Jesus taught the parable of the unmerciful servant. As a side note, it is well for us modern readers to remember that Jesus surely knew from the beginning that His teachings would be recorded and passed on to hundreds of generations to come. They would eventually be studied by millions of people down through centuries of time and across the breadth of the whole world. So in a very real way, Jesus's admonition to forgive seventy times seven was not for Peter alone.

Because of the length and complexity of this parable, we shall study it in pieces, inserting our analysis as we go.

THE PARABLE

Therefore is the kingdom of heaven likened unto a certain king, which would take account of his servants. And when he had begun to reckon, one was brought unto him, which owed him ten thousand talents. But forasmuch as he had not to pay, his lord commanded him to be sold, and his wife, and children, and all that he had, and payment to be made.

The servant therefore fell down, and worshiped him, saying, Lord, have patience with me, and I will pay thee all. Then the lord of that servant was moved with compassion, and loosed him, and forgave him the debt. (Matthew 18:23–27)

ANALYSIS

This parable, which is one of the longer parables of the New Testament, is an outstanding example of how the parables of Jesus are literary masterpieces. Note how clearly the character and personality of the people in this story are given in such a few words. It is quite amazing how vividly we can picture this happening.

Since we no longer trade in talents, we need a better idea of just how much money we are talking about here in the parable. Though it is difficult to determine the precise equivalent values between their system and ours, we have a pretty good idea of how much one talent was worth in terms of our modern buying power. But keep in mind that what is most important in this analysis is not the amounts of money, but the difference between the first debt and the second. Therein is the power of the lesson Jesus taught.

At the time of Jesus there were various forms of money, all of which were based on precious metals. Metal coins were used in everyday transactions. As far as we know there was no paper currency. And the value of each piece was based on its weight, which ranged from coins about the size of our dime to heavy blocks of precious or semiprecious metals known as talents. One Bible scholar gives us an insight into the worth of a talent:

[A] talent . . . was the largest weight among the Hebrews, . . . whether gold, silver, lead, bronze, or iron. The talent was used by various nations, and . . . it is perhaps impossible to determine if the Hebrews had one talent only or several. . . . A talent seems to have been a full weight for an able man to carry. (Merrill F. Unger, *Unger's Bible Dictionary*, 722)

Scholars suggest that the various talents ran between about forty to ninety of our pounds, but on average were more likely about sixty-five pounds. Talents of gold were most frequently mentioned in the ancient records, so we shall assume the ten thousand talents in the parable were gold talents as well.

In recent decades, the price of gold in our modern world has skyrocketed. Though it fluctuates, we could use a possible modern equivalent of $500 per ounce of gold.

- One talent of gold weighing 65 pounds would be 1,040 ounces.
- At $500 per ounce, one talent would be worth $520,000!
- Ten thousand talents would be worth $5.2 billion dollars!

That sum is such a staggering amount it is almost inconceivable how a household servant could ever have racked up that much debt. Because of the enormity of the debt, some scholars have suggested that his master was actually a king, and the first servant was likely a government servant of high rank, similar to ministers of state or what we call secretaries of state in America. This would better explain how a servant could have gotten himself into such a massive debt.

What makes this story all the more stunning is when we better appreciate not just the sums involved, but the consequences of the punishment. When the king threatened to put the servant *and his family* in prison until the debt was paid, the servant fell down at the feet of the king and begged for mercy, saying, "Lord, have patience with me and I will pay thee all." How much patience was he asking for?

Let's ignore for a minute that this man had no means to pay the king back, and suppose that he offered to repay the debt at the rate of $5,000 per day. That's a payment of $35,000 per week, or about $150,000 a month. Or a mere $1.8 million each year! We know that this is an impossibly high rate, but we use it to show just how much "patience" the king would need to wait for his debt to be paid.

If the servant started payments at $5,000 per day starting on the day that Lehi left Jerusalem (around 600 BC), and had paid that amount every day since that time—that's 2,621 years at the time of this writing—even so, at this point, the servant would still owe the king $376,000,000! Which would take him another two hundred and nine years to pay off. And all of that is calculated without interest!

It is a stunning thought. But even more staggering is what happened next. The king took pity on the man and essentially said, "Oh, well. It's only ten thousand talents. Let's just write it off."

Unbelievable!

Peter must have been stunned with what Jesus was telling him. But what followed next was even more surprising.

THE PARABLE (CONT.)

But the same servant went out, and found one of his fellowservants, which owed him an hundred pence: and he laid hands on him, and took him by the throat, saying, Pay me that thou owest. And his fellowservant fell down at his feet, and besought him, saying, Have patience with me, and I will pay thee all. And he would not: but went and cast him into prison, till he should pay the debt. (Matthew 18:28–30)

ANALYSIS (CONT.)

What happened next in the parable is equally stunning. "The same servant *went out and found* his fellow servant." One would expect that after what had just happened, the first servant would be so overwhelmed with joy at his own good fortune that he would race home to share the news with his wife and family, for they too were facing imprisonment. But no. His first thought was to find a fellow servant who owed him a debt.

After what had just happened, one would hope that the first servant would have gone to find him to share the incredible news. To have someone to rejoice with him. But not so. His purpose is quite the opposite. This man owes him a hundred pence. Note the details of the exchange, which reveal the character of this first servant. He takes him by the throat. What? He doesn't even share his good news! Unbelievable! How vivid is that imagery!

But there is more: The second servant also begged for mercy. And his words? "Have patience with me and I shall pay thee all"— sound familiar? Yes! The second servant used identical language to the first to plead his cause. That alone should have brought the first man up short.

How do the two debts compare? That too is significant. A

"pence" was the Roman *denarius*, a silver coin commonly used in the Holy Land at that time. We don't know exactly what its equivalent would be in our currency today, but we do know that it was the sum given to a laborer for one twelve-hour day of work (see the parable of the laborers in the vineyard), or about $180 in today's economy. But this servant owed the other a *hundred* pence, or about $18,000 in our day.

Clearly this was not an insignificant amount. But, to keep things in perspective, the ten thousand talents that the first servant had just had been forgiven is about 290 times greater that what his fellow servant owed him!

THE PARABLE (CONT.)

So when his fellowservants saw what was done, they were very sorry, and came and told unto their lord all that was done. Then his lord, after that he had called him, said unto him, O thou wicked servant, I forgave thee all that debt, because thou desiredst me: Shouldest not thou also have had compassion on thy fellowservant, even as I had pity on thee?

And his lord was wroth, and delivered him to the tormentors, till he should pay all that was due unto him. So likewise shall my heavenly Father do also unto you, if ye from your hearts forgive not every one his brother their trespasses. (Matthew 18:31–35)

APPLICATION

There is not much subtlety in the message of this parable. There seems to be a reason why the debt owed to the king by the first servant was so astronomically high. Just as there was a reason why the second debt was such a tiny fraction of the first. To better understand why this was so, let us once again set up the parallel structure that is the trademark of the parables of Jesus.

The king	Ultimately this would represent the Father and His Son.
The first servant	Humans in general, with all of their imperfection, pettiness, selfishness, etc.
Ten thousand talents	An indication of how frequently we sin or transgress and offend God. To illustrate that better, here are two depressing questions. If we define sin and transgression as anything we *think*, *do*, or *say* that is offensive to God, then (1) How many times have we sinned or transgressed in this life? (2) When was the *last time* that we did something that offended God in any degree? It is especially depressing to realize that in most cases, the answer to the second question would be "Today."
Complete forgiveness of first debt	God has told us that if we repent, are baptized and receive the gift of the Holy Ghost, and strive to live the gospel in our lives, then all of our past sins, weaknesses, mistakes, and transgressions will be forgiven. Through the Atonement of Jesus Christ, all can be forgiven and set aside at the Judgment.
The second servant	Our fellow men and women, i.e., all of the human race. All are also in debt just as we are.

A hundred pence	The transgressions and wrongs that others have done to us. While some of those wrongs may be deep and devastating, compared to the total debt we owe to the "King," they are a pittance, a tiny fraction of the greater debt.
No forgiveness of the second debt	Someone once defined human nature in this terse way: "We blame others for their wrong actions, but justify ourselves for our good intentions." The first servant is a stunning example of that homily.

The scriptures teach us how commonly sin and transgression are part of the human experience. Here are just a few examples:

- *"All* have sinned, and come short of the glory of God" (Romans 3:23; emphasis added).[2] Christ is the only exception to that.

- "I cannot tell you all the things whereby ye may commit sin; for there are divers ways and means, even so many that I cannot number them" (Mosiah 4:29).

- "The Lord cannot look upon sin with the least degree of allowance" (Alma 45:16).

- "Ye ought to forgive one another; for he that forgiveth not his brother his trespasses standeth condemned before the Lord; *for there remaineth in him the greater sin.* I, the Lord, will forgive whom I will forgive, but of you it is required to forgive all men (D&C 64:9–10; emphasis added).

- "Your iniquities have separated between you and your God, and your sins have hid his face from you, that he will not hear" (Isaiah 59:2).

And yet, here are the promises of the King of Glory to His servants, which are the equivalents to the forgiveness of our ten-thousand-talent debt:

- "Come, my brethren, every one that thirsteth, come ye to the waters; and he that hath no money, come buy and eat; yea, come buy wine and milk without money and without price" (2 Nephi 9:50).

- "Behold, doth he cry unto any, saying: Depart from me? Behold, I say unto you, Nay; but he saith: Come unto me all ye ends of the earth, buy milk and honey, without money and without price" (2 Nephi 26:25).

In one of the most intimate revelations from our Savior, He explained to us how it is that He can redeem our sins—because He paid the price for them as if He had committed them, and that created such agony of body and soul that He bled at every pore.

I command you to repent—repent, lest I smite you by the rod of my mouth, and by my wrath, and by my anger, and your sufferings be sore—how sore you know not, how exquisite you know not, yea, how hard to bear you know not. For behold, I, God, have suffered these things for all, that they might not suffer if they would repent; But if they would not repent they must suffer even as I; Which suffering caused myself, even God, the greatest of all, to tremble because of pain, and to bleed at every pore, and to suffer both body and spirit—and would that I might not drink the bitter cup, and shrink—Nevertheless, glory be to the Father, and I partook and finished my preparations unto the children of men. Wherefore, I command you again to repent, lest I humble you with my almighty power; and that you confess your sins, lest you suffer these punishments of which I have spoken. (D&C 19:15–20)

Again in our dispensation, Jesus spoke with equal clarity about our responsibility to forgive:

My disciples, in days of old, sought occasion against one another and forgave not one another in their hearts; and for this evil they were afflicted and sorely chastened. Wherefore, I say unto you, that ye ought to forgive one another; for he that forgiveth not his brother his trespasses standeth condemned before the Lord; for there remaineth in him the greater sin. I, the Lord, will forgive whom I will forgive, but of you it is required to forgive all men. And ye ought to say in your hearts—let God judge between me and thee, and reward thee according to thy deeds. (D&C 64:8–11)

These are the lessons taught by our Savior through the parable of the unmerciful servant. How ironic that the one was forgiven by a king, then refused to forgive a fellow servant. Are we sometimes guilty of that? Seeking tolerance and forgiveness for our foolish decisions from our King, even as we are filled with anger, bitterness, and even hatred for much slighter offenses.

Three scriptures are especially pertinent as we close this study of the unmerciful servant.

"I, the Lord, will forgive whom I will forgive, but of you it is required to forgive all men" (D&C 64:10).

"Though your sins be as scarlet, they shall be as white as snow; though they be red like crimson, they shall be as wool" (Isaiah 1:18).

"Behold, he who has repented of his sins, the same is forgiven, and I, the Lord, remember them no more" (D&C 58:42).

Those are the promises of the Father to His children through His Son. This is our Heavenly King making these promises to His imperfect children. How can we not be so filled with gratitude for that miracle that we find that same forgiving spirit for those who have trespassed against us?

Sister Susan H. Porter, serving as First Counselor in the Primary General Presidency, spoke on this theme in general conference of October 2021.

> God's love is not found in the *circumstances* of our lives *but in His presence in our lives.* We know of His love when we receive strength beyond our own and when His Spirit brings peace, comfort, and direction. . . . May we open our hearts to receive the pure love that God has for us and then shed forth His love in all we do and are. ("God's Love: The Most Joyous to the Soul," *Liahona,* November 2021; emphasis added)

NOTES

1. This term could include a brother in the Church and not only a member of the family.

2. Children who have not yet reached the age of accountability may do some things that are selfish, wrong, or hurtful, but those are not counted as sins against them because they don't yet have sufficient understanding.

Chapter 6

The Unjust Judge

CONTEXT AND SETTING

Luke is the only writer to include this parable in his Gospel. This was not long before Jesus would go to Jerusalem for Passover and there be arrested, tried, and crucified. The chapter immediately preceding this parable (Luke 17) describes Jesus as He taught the people and worked miracles among them.

However, a good part of that chapter focuses on how Jesus responded to some of the Pharisees who demanded to know when the kingdom of God would come. Jesus spoke often of this, but He told these haughty Pharisees that the kingdom was not going to come "with observation," i.e., simply because people were watching and waiting for a set time or certain specific indicators. He warned them that it would come unexpectedly and catch many people unprepared, eating and drinking and marrying as if life were perfectly normal (see Luke 17:20–31).

In this teaching moment, Jesus next used the examples of Noah and the flood and Lot and the destruction of Sodom and Gomorrah to emphasize His point. These are two of the most disastrous events in the history of the covenant people. Both came swiftly and when most of the people were not prepared. Both are examples of how quickly disaster can strike. Jesus then warned His listeners that another disaster was coming in which people would have to flee so rapidly that if they turned back to get things from their homes they could be caught up in it.

This seems to be a reference to the Jewish rebellion against Rome, AD 65–72. When the Romans responded, hundreds of thousands were killed, the suffering through the siege and the famine it brought with it was horrific, and about 900,000 Jews were sold into slavery. It was another massive catastrophe. Jesus had prophesied of this disastrous time in the Olivet Discourse (see Matthew 24:15–22; see also JS—M 1:12–22) about thirty-three years before it began. Some Jews who had converted to Christianity remembered His prophecy and fled to safety and were saved.

This theme is what immediately preceded Jesus giving the parable of the unjust judge. While the parable does not seem to have a direct connection to Jesus's warning about coming disaster, the principle taught in the parable—how to get answers to our prayers—would certainly be an important one to remember in times of great upheaval and catastrophic disasters, as well as in everyday life.

Luke opens the parable with these words: "And he spake a parable unto them to this end, that men ought always to pray, and not to faint. . . ." (Luke 18:1). That wording could suggest that this summary of the purpose of the parable comes from Luke, not the Savior. However, the next word, "Saying," clearly shows that it is Jesus who then gives the parable. However, Luke's insight into the purpose of the parable is an important key for understanding it.

That the primary focus of the parable is on prayer is very clear. And since prayer is so integral to discipleship, this short but powerful parable has great value for our day.

The parable is quite short, only five verses. Yet note again the insights Jesus gives into the characters of the judge and the widow, the only two people in the story. His description of each gives us another good example of why the parables are considered literary treasures and are as valuable and relevant for our day as they were when given more than two thousand years ago.

THE PARABLE

And he spake a parable unto them to this end, that men ought always to pray, and not to faint;[1] Saying, There was in a city a judge, which feared not God, neither regarded man.

And there was a widow in that city; and she came unto him, saying, Avenge me of mine adversary. And he would not for a while: but afterward he said within himself, Though I fear not God, nor regard man; Yet because this widow troubleth me, I will avenge her, lest by her continual coming she weary me. And the Lord said, Hear what the unjust judge saith. (Luke 18:1–6)

Before analyzing the parable, note another unusual aspect. Not only are we given the lesson of the parable before Jesus shared it, but He also emphatically reemphasized the message a second time when He finished:

And the Lord said, Hear what the unjust judge saith. And shall not God avenge his own elect, which cry day and night unto him, though he bear long with them? I tell you that he will avenge them speedily. Nevertheless when the Son of man cometh, shall he find faith on the earth? (Luke 18:6–8)

ANALYSIS

As has been noted before, Jesus often opened His parables with, "And the kingdom of heaven is likened unto. . . ." He doesn't say that here, but the parable teaches us to pray earnestly to strengthen our relationship with God, or, in other words, it teaches how to qualify for the kingdom of heaven.

The principle taught in the parable is called "importuning." From that, some have given this parable another name: the parable of the importunate woman. That word is not found in the Bible, but it is a word that aptly describes the widow in the parable. *Importune* comes from a Latin word meaning "to make oneself troublesome." Other words might include *persevere, pester,* or *annoy.*

Though the judge is one of the two key characters in this short tale, it is the woman who becomes the model of persistence as she seeks justice from him and refuses to give up.

Let us begin our analysis of the parable by taking a closer look at the two individuals in the parable. Jesus described the judge as a man "which feared not God, neither regarded man" (Luke 18:2). Clearly, this judge was tough-minded, hard-hearted, and uncaring. For him to say "I fear not God" seems to suggest that he was not a deeply religious man. "Neither regarded man" also tells us that he was basically heartless. His arrogance has convinced him that there is no one that can influence him against his will, especially not a pitiful old widow. We could say that in his towering arrogance, he did *what* he wanted to do, *when* and *how* he wanted to do it (or not do it), and took pride in his reputation as being heartless.

Hold that thought for a moment as we consider this judge from a gospel point of view. Throughout all four of the standard works we find the Lord calling on His people to pay attention to two groups who are in need of special care: widows and orphans and the poor and needy. Here are just a few examples to illustrate:

- "Ye shall not afflict any widow, or fatherless child" (Exodus 22:22).
- "Learn to do well; seek judgment, relieve the oppressed, judge the fatherless, plead for the widow" (Isaiah 1:17).

- "Woe unto you, scribes and Pharisees, hypocrites! for ye devour widows' houses, and for a pretense make long prayer: therefore ye shall receive the greater damnation" (Matthew 23:14).
- "King Limhi commanded that every man should impart to the support of the widows and their children, that they might not perish with hunger" (Mosiah 21:17).
- "I will come near to you to judgment; and I will be a swift witness against . . . those that oppress the hireling in his wages, the widow and the fatherless, . . . saith the Lord of Hosts" (3 Nephi 24:5).
- "The [bishop's] storehouse shall be kept by the consecrations of the church; and widows and orphans shall be provided for, as also the poor" (D&C 83:6).

Though we are not told in the parable what the widow's grievance was, the implication is that it was very important to her. It may be that the judge was the one who ruled against her in court. But her efforts to appeal to his better nature are of no avail. In his hierarchy of important people in his life, this annoying widow was a nobody, a cipher not worthy of the slightest concern or sympathy.

So what was it that finally changed his mind and caused him to relent? *Importuning!*

If we were to speculate on the judge's feelings based on that brief but powerful description of his character, his reasoning may have gone something like this:

"I've made my ruling in this case and I stand by it. So what if that old crone is upset with me? That happens all the time. She's not a person with any influence. She certainly has no money to give me under the table. Nor does she have anyone of influence to speak for her.

"And I am certainly not worried that some supposed god in heaven will hurl down thunderbolts to punish me. And yet. . . .

"She's not giving up. This has been going on for weeks now. Every time I come out of the courthouse there she is on the steps, wailing and crying out for mercy. She's outside my house each morning, telling anyone who will listen what a cold and wicked man I am. I've had to take my phone off the hook, lock my doors, and turn off the internet. It's embarrassing. Everybody looks at me like I'm some kind of pariah.

"So even though I don't have the slightest touch of compassion for her, and while there's no compelling reason why I *have* to do this, I'm going to give her what she wants. That's the only way I'm going to get any peace."

And so he gives in to her pleadings.

Jesus then closed the parable with an appeal to His listeners, including the Pharisees. "Hear what the unjust judge saith!" (Luke 18:6). Or in our plainer words, "Pay attention; learn a lesson from this woman's persistence and the judge's response to it."

Before turning to the application of this parable in our lives, there is one other unusual aspect about it to note. It is quoted word for word in a modern revelation given to the Prophet Joseph Smith. On July 20, 1831, Joseph Smith, other Church leaders, and a small body of members of the Church were gathered in Jackson County, Missouri. There the Lord revealed to them the location of the Land of Zion spoken of by many of the ancient prophets (see D&C 57:3). This was electrifying news to the fledgling Church, and a call went out to some of the Saints to gather to Missouri and begin building up Zion as the prophets had foretold millennia before.

Many responded, and soon there was a strong Latter-day Saint community in that area. But they quickly ran into intense opposition from the locals. Eventually, in the summer and fall of 1833, the hatred and animosity of the Missourians exploded into open warfare. Several Saints were killed, and others suffered greatly as they were driven out of Jackson County completely (see *Saints: The Story of the Church of Jesus Christ in the Latter Days, vol. 1, The Standard of Truth, 1815–1846 [2018]*, chapters 12–17).

In response to this travesty of justice, the Lord gave another revelation to Joseph, stating that part of this tragedy had come because the members had not been faithful to their commitments to their calling as Saints (see D&C 101:1–8). But the Lord also noted that these actions were in contradiction to the Constitution of the United States established by the founding fathers just a few decades before. The Lord said through Joseph Smith, "It is my will that they should continue to *importune* for redress, and redemption, by the hands of those who are placed as rulers and are in authority over you" (D&C 101:76; emphasis added).

Under Joseph Smith's direction, the leaders of the Church gathered evidence and took depositions from those who had suffered and began the process of petitioning for justice. In that same revelation, the Lord cited the parable of the unjust judge:

> And for this purpose have I established the Constitution of this land, by the hands of wise men whom I raised up unto this very purpose, and redeemed the land by the shedding of blood. Now, unto what shall I liken the children of Zion? I will liken them unto the parable of the woman and the unjust judge, for men ought always to pray and not to faint, which saith— (D&C 101:80–81)

The Lord then quoted the parable exactly as it is found in Luke's account, but added this further admonition:

> Thus will I liken the children of Zion. Let them importune at the feet of the judge; And if he heed them not, let them importune at the feet of the governor; And if the governor heed them not, let them importune at the feet

of the president; And if the president heed them not, then will the Lord arise and come forth out of his hiding place, and in his fury vex the nation; And in his hot displeasure, and in his fierce anger, in his time, will cut off those wicked, unfaithful, and unjust stewards, and appoint them their portion among hypocrites, and unbelievers; even in outer darkness, where there is weeping, and wailing, and gnashing of teeth. (D&C 101:85–91)

Over the next few years, the Saints gathered evidence and sent it to Washington, presenting their cause to both houses of Congress. But it was to no avail. The lawmakers of that day said that while they were sympathetic to the cause of the Saints, they could do nothing for them since this was not a federal matter. (What a shabby dodge that was.) The first ten amendments added to the Constitution several important rights of the federal government. One of those ten amendments reads, "Congress shall make no law respecting an establishment of religion, or prohibiting the free exercise thereof."

After receiving no action from Congress, in 1839, the Prophet finally got an audience with Martin Van Buren, president of the United States. His response was that of the consummate politician, a practice called political expediency: "I can do nothing for you, gentlemen. If I were for you, I should go against the whole state of Missouri, and that state would go against me in the next election" (*Saints, vol. 1*, 408).

APPLICATION

There are two somewhat troublesome aspects in the counsel of Jesus to importune the Lord in our prayers. First, some might think that because the widow petitioned the judge for relief from her problem, that the judge is likened unto our Heavenly Father, to whom we pray. But that cannot be, for the judge is a proud and wicked man, and our Father is perfect in every aspect of His character and attributes.

Second, in the structure of the story, the central character is not the judge. He is only a player. It is the widow *who provides the model for us of what Jesus was teaching.* Remember, the Savior told His listeners what the moral of the story was before He told the story. It was that "men ought always to pray and not to faint." That's a key to understanding the parable.

What does the judge teach us about prayer? Absolutely nothing. It is the widow that we are to emulate, not the judge. And note that it is not the prayers of the widow that are praised. There is no mention of her praying. She probably did, but it doesn't say so. Then what does the Lord praise? *Her persistence!*

And that is the lesson the Lord was teaching all of us. When we think about it, prayer itself is an amazing gift we imperfect humans are given by our perfect Heavenly Father. We can approach Him any time of the day or night, any time in the year, about anything that is bothering us. And we are invited to ask for His help in solving our problems. That is amazing when we compare that to our earthly communications. When we pray we never get a busy signal. We never get a recording telling us to call back during business hours. We are not put on hold. There are no holidays when the office is closed. The line is available any time, from any place in the world, to any person, in any language. That is really quite astonishing!

But there is one thing that we humans often tend to overlook in this remarkable privilege that is ours. It is this: Yes, we can call on God at any time and present any question or problem to Him. But it is not our privilege to tell God *how* to solve our problem, nor *when.* And as we learn more about this amazing opportunity we call prayer, it appears from the parable that the Lord wants us to understand a simple principle about prayer that is often overlooked by

His children: Just because there is no answer does not automatically mean that the answer is no!

In the parable, the widow demonstrates this principle. But there's a logical dilemma in that concept. We believe that God is omniscient, i.e., that He knows all things. To put it more plainly, there is no way or time that we kneel in prayer, pour out our heart to God, telling Him what our troubles and concerns are, and have Him say, "*Oh,* I didn't know that." In one way, it seems like we should just be able to kneel and say, "Heavenly Father, Thou knowest what my needs are, and how best to fill them. And the sooner the better would be nice."

So why would Jesus ask that we importune the Father in our prayers until, like the unjust judge, He seems to throw up His hands in exasperation and gives us what we are asking for?

One possible answer is found in the parable. Since we accept the premise that Heavenly Father, Jesus, and the Holy Spirit are perfect in every way, if we feel that God isn't answering us, in one way or another the problem lies with us, not with Him. So let's think that through more carefully.

Let's say that we face some kind of serious challenge in our lives, something we desperately need God's help with. So we earnestly begin to pray for His blessings. Nothing happens. So what do we do? We pray more earnestly; maybe we add fasting to our prayers. We ask ourselves, "What more can I do to call down the powers of heaven in my life?"

Incidentally, some take another path, saying, "He's not answering me. Therefore, He isn't there, He doesn't care, or He can't fix my problem." And they turn away from prayer, and often turn away from God as well.

But let's speak of those who don't take that path. What do we do when no answer comes? Here are some possibilities. In our wonderings of why nothing is happening, we begin to look inwardly. We might call this taking personal inventory. We decide to be more active in those things that bring the Spirit into our lives. We study the scriptures more diligently. We may remember that we are late in paying our tithing and send it in immediately. We strive to be more attentive and loving to our families or to serve more diligently in our ministering callings. And all the time, as we continue pleading for the Father to intervene in our behalf, we are beginning to express our willingness to accept His will over our own. But then, still nothing happens. Nothing changes. And we ask, "Why? Why isn't God answering me?"

That is a very important question in our spiritual growth. And there are at least four answers we might come up with in response to that question:

- *God is answering me, but the answer is no.* For some reason, He doesn't want me to have what I'm seeking. And knowing that His love for me is perfect, I have to assume He has good reason for not answering. There are times when "no" *is* the answer.

- *The problem here is not with me, but with God.* This answer typically shows a lack of understanding about God, His nature, and how He works. In our spiritual immaturity, we petulantly decide that He doesn't hear us. Or, if He does, He doesn't care what's happening to us. Too often, in this myopic view of our relationship to Him, in our frustration we decide that if He's going to be that way, then we're done with Him. We'll stop praying. That will show Him! For that matter, we might ask, what if there is no God at all? What if I am totally on my own in this?

- *The problem is with me.* We accept our weaknesses and follies, our inadequacies and limitations. And we begin a self-evaluation process, asking questions like: What am I doing wrong? Or what am I *not* doing? What do I need to do to create deeper spiritual power in my life? Or, what do I need to eliminate from my life that is blocking this from happening? How do I make those changes? These questions become an important spiritual turning point in our lives, for now we have humbled ourselves and earnestly begin the process of change. We pay our delinquent tithing, attend church more regularly, serve in our calling more diligently. We move from *reading* the scriptures *to studying and pondering* them. In other words, the fact that our Father in Heaven chooses to hold back in answering our prayers can become a powerful agent of change in our lives, the personal change that we call repentance.

- *Just because there is no answer now, doesn't mean that the answer is "no."* That is a mistake we often make. We might assume that no answer is a "no" answer. This is closely related to the previous point. One of the important acts in developing and deepening our faith is to trust in His perfection, trust in His love, trust that He knows far better than we do what is best for us, and how and when to answer our prayers. And these are just a few of the possibilities. There could be a host of reasons for Him holding back the blessings for a time. Maybe certain conditions have to be met first, or certain individuals may need to be brought into our lives. He may withhold His answer for a time to make us stretch spiritually.

When we undertake what we could call this "personal spiritual inventory" and ask ourselves what is hampering the flow of revelation, then we begin to humble ourselves, to institute change. We begin to "fix" whatever it is that is blocking our communication with Him.

And the process of searching, yearning, and undertaking a personal self-inventory is so beneficial to our spiritual growth that the Lord says, "Be patient. I am here. And I will give you the righteous desires of your heart. But not yet! You need this opportunity to grow and learn."

Elder Neal A. Maxwell of the Quorum of the Twelve Apostles called such times as these we have just described as "divine tutorials."

In no dimension of the divine personality of Jesus Christ do we see His love any more fully expressed than in the divine tutorials given especially to His friends. . . . He would not deny these enriching but stretching divine tutorials to any who follow Him. . . . *Perhaps these divine tutorials carry such a high priority because the more we are fully developed here, the more chores and opportunities we can be given in the world to come.* (Neal A. Maxwell, *Even as I Am*, 42, 46; emphasis added)

Elder Maxwell also gave us another a great insight on this process we call personal revelation and the development of our faith. "President Boyd K. Packer has counseled us that often when we receive guidance from the Holy Ghost, *we get direction without explanation*" (*The Promise of Discipleship*, 99–100; emphasis added).

That is a simple but profound thought. Remember Nephi's experience in getting the brass plates from Laban? That is a perfect example of this principle. After finding a safe place in the wilderness, Lehi was directed by the Lord to send his sons back to Jerusalem for the brass plates. They set off, likely assuming that since God had required it that it was going to be an easy task. Instead, Laban threw them out and tried to kill them. Laman and Lemuel immediately wanted to give up, but Nephi wouldn't do that. When they refused to go back, he decided to go back on his own. Note how he describes what followed: "I was led by the Spirit, *not knowing beforehand* the things which I should do. Nevertheless, I went forth" (1 Nephi 4:6–7; emphasis added).

This is a classic example of getting direction without confirmation. Nephi moved forward purely on faith, very likely wondering if this was going to cost him his life. But once he acted on that faith, then the answer came. This is often how the Lord works with us. But, some would ask, why didn't the Lord just tell Nephi that He was going to deliver Laban into his hands and that all would be all right? We don't know all of God's purposes, but as things developed, we see that one very important thing happened in Nephi's young life that would bless him through all the years to come: he learned that God is there! He does hear and answer our prayers, just not always when and how we hoped or thought He would.

President Russell M. Nelson once spoke on two aspects of our spiritual growth: Our *perception* and the Lord's *perspective.*

> Imagine, if you will, a pair of powerful binoculars. Two separate optical systems are joined together with a gear to focus two independent images into one three-dimensional view. To apply this analogy, let the scene on the left side of your binoculars represent *your perception* of your task. Let the picture on the right side represent the *Lord's* perspective of your task—the portion of His plan He has entrusted to you. Now, connect your system to His. By mental adjustment, fuse your focus. Something wonderful happens. Your vision and His are now the same. You have developed an "eye single to the glory of God" (D&C 4:5; see also Mormon 8:15). With that perspective, look upward—above and beyond mundane things about you. The Lord said, "Look unto me in every thought" (D&C 6:36). That special vision will also help clarify your wishes when they may be

a bit fuzzy and out of focus with God's hopes for your divine destiny. Indeed, the precise challenge you regard now as "impossible" may be the very refinement you need, in His eye. (*Teachings*, 253)

In this short but wonderful parable about an unjust, unmerciful judge and a sorrowing widow who would not give up, we are taught a powerful principle about strengthening our relationship and our communication with our Heavenly Father and His most beloved Son.

The Prophet Joseph Smith, after spending months in the hellhole of Liberty Jail while his people were being driven out of Missouri in the dead of winter, cried out in an agony of not understanding: "O God! Where art thou? And where is the pavilion that covereth thy hiding place? How long shall thy hand be stayed?" (D&C 121:1–2).

And the most heart-wrenching plea of all came from the only perfect Being to ever come to this earth. Here is the cry that came from Jesus as He hung in agony on the cross: "My God, my God! Why hast thou forsaken me?" (Matthew 27:46). In this case, what was required of the Savior evidently could not be set aside. President James E. Faust of the First Presidency said this about that terrible moment at Calvary:

> He was led to Golgotha, where nails were driven into His hands and feet. He hung in agony for hours on a wooden cross. . . . Darkness came, and "about the ninth hour Jesus cried with a loud voice, saying, Eli, Eli, lama sabachthani? that is to say, My God, my God, why hast thou forsaken me?" No one could help Him; He was treading the winepress alone. ("The Atonement: Our Greatest Hope," *Ensign*, November 2001)

These powerful examples are evidence that confirms that sometimes "no answer" is not the same as a "no" answer. That principle is taught in the parable of the unjust judge. If we give up too soon, we may miss out on some of the most important spiritual training that God has to offer us.

One last thought on this principle, and it has to do with patience in spiritual things. Moroni taught us this principle in simple clarity. "And now, I, Moroni, would speak somewhat concerning these things; I would show unto the world that *faith is things which are hoped for and not seen*; wherefore, *dispute not because ye see not, for ye receive no witness until after the trial of your faith*" (Ether 12:6; emphasis added).

That is the lesson of the parable of the unjust judge. I close this chapter with this wonderful invitation from the Savior Himself:

"Behold, I stand at the door and knock: if any man hear my voice and open the door, I will come in to him, and will sup with him, and he with me, . . . He that hath an ear, let him hear what the Spirit saith" (Revelation 3:20, 22).

NOTES

1. The old English word here does not mean to lose consciousness, rather to give up too soon, to quit, to turn away from a task.

Chapter 7

The Pharisee *and the* Publican;
The Two Sons

This chapter will be somewhat different than previous chapters. To this point, each parable, along with its context and setting, analysis, and application, has been treated in a separate chapter. In this chapter we shall examine two parables, both of which teach us about the covenants we make with the Father and the Son, and how keeping those covenants helps us to become more faithful servants. Each of the parables is brief, but in that simplicity we find some important lessons on how to become true disciples of the Master.

CONTEXT AND SETTING: THE PHARISEE AND THE PUBLICAN

In the previous chapter, we studied the parable of the unjust judge. That is the immediate context for this parable, for this short parable immediately followed that parable with no preamble or introduction. Consider that placement for a moment. Jesus taught that we should pray and not give up, which is a powerful principle not only about prayer but also about receiving personal revelation.

What followed was another lesson on prayer, but not on the nature of prayer, but on two examples of how we pray.

It is an interesting juxtaposition. In the parable of the unjust judge, Jesus taught the importance of importuning in our prayers. Now He describes another principle that impacts how effective our prayers may be. It is the principle of humility. Luke tells us that Jesus gave this parable to a specific group. "And he spake this parable unto certain which *trusted in themselves that they were righteous, and despised others*" (Luke 18:9; emphasis added). Clearly, that is the opposite of humility.

THE PARABLE

Two men went up into the temple to pray; the one a Pharisee, and the other a publican. The Pharisee stood and prayed thus with himself, God, I thank thee, that I am not as other men are, extortioners, unjust, adulterers, or even as this publican. I fast twice in the week, I give tithes of all that I possess.

And the publican, standing afar off, would not lift up so much as his eyes unto heaven, but smote upon his breast, saying, God be merciful to me a sinner. (Luke 18:10–13)

ANALYSIS

To more fully appreciate the message of the parable, we need to have a better understanding of who the two men in the parable were and why Jesus chose them as examples. To do so, we need to briefly review some history of the house of Israel.

It all began with Abraham and his wife Sarah about 2000 BC. God made a covenant with Abraham that the covenant people should come through his lineage. One of Abraham's grandsons was Jacob, whose name was changed to Israel. Jacob had twelve sons who became the twelve tribes of Israel. Joseph, second to youngest, was hated by his brothers, and they sold him as a slave and he was taken to Egypt. There, through his faithfulness, he rose to be vice-regent to the pharaoh. When a great famine struck the region, Jacob and the rest of his family came to Egypt and the whole family was reunited.

After Joseph's death, a new Pharaoh rose to power and enslaved the Israelites and put them into bondage, where they remained for the next four hundred years. God then raised up Moses, who led the children of Israel out of bondage into the wilderness. Because they were not spiritually ready to enter the promised land, they wandered in the wilderness for forty years. Finally, under the leadership of Joshua, the Israelites entered the promised land and conquered most of the tribes living there. They divided up the land between the tribes, and the promised land became the land of Israel.

Unfortunately, as the centuries passed, more and more the people of Israel turned away from their faith and embraced the idol worship that was prevalent there. As the wickedness increased, eventually the twelve tribes divided into two kingdoms—the kingdom of Israel (ten tribes) and kingdom of Judah (two tribes). Though there were times of righteousness and peace, both kingdoms kept moving further and further away from their original faith and, as a result, more and more lost God's protective power.

In AD 721, the Northern Kingdom was invaded by the Assyrian Empire. Many were killed and the rest were taken captive back to Assyria. They assimilated into the Assyrian culture and religion and eventually lost their identity and never returned to their homeland.

When that disaster happened, the Southern Kingdom turned back to God, and the people were not taken captive at that time. But they too eventually abandoned their faith, and in 587 BC they were captured by the Babylonians and also taken away into slavery. (It was a few years before this time that Lehi and his family were warned by God and left the Middle East and sailed to the Americas.)

About seventy years later, some of the captive Jews in Babylon were allowed to return to their homeland. Most of the others had assimilated into Babylonian society by that point, and, like the Northern Kingdom, ceased to be identified as Israelites any longer. But those who returned were determined to stay faithful to their God.

From that time to the time of Jesus Christ, the promised land was under the dominion of various empires except for one short period of independence. By New Testament times, the empire that ruled the world, including the province of Judea, was Rome. By that time much of the house of Israel had gone into another form of apostasy. They still lived under the law of Moses, but pride and the quest for worldly wealth permeated much of their society. There were three main religious groups by that time. The first were the Sadducees, who were of the priestly class and controlled the temple and its enormous revenues. Ironically, they were more secular than religious.

The other two main groups, the scribes and the Pharisees, were closely related in their beliefs. They were essentially the same group of people, but some Pharisees were experts in the law of Moses and served much the same role as attorneys in our day. We often see the two names linked together in the New Testament.

Some of the Jews who had returned from Babylon believed that their national tragedy was the direct result of their turning away from the law of Moses. They determined to live more faithfully so it wouldn't happen again. The scribes—so called because they could read and write—decided to create rules and requirements that would help the people keep the law of Moses. They joined with Pharisees in their obsession with the minutia of the law rather than the spirit. But they too, over the centuries, had become rich, powerful, and obsessed with living the law perfectly. By the time of Christ, they were one of the most numerous and influential of the Jewish religious sects.

When Jesus came and began teaching the people the simple principles of the gospel, He often infuriated the scribes and the Pharisees because He saw through their hypocrisy and openly condemned their pride and their wickedness. One of the two in this parable was a Pharisee.

The other person described in the parable was a publican. This title was not directly related to religion. Under the heel of Rome, the province of Judea was allowed to govern itself, but under the close supervision of the Romans. The Romans, like all empires, taxed their subjects heavily. But the Romans did not do so directly. Ever practical, the Romans devised a simple and workable way to collect taxes in the provinces. They hired local citizens as their tax assessors/ collectors and let them add enough surcharge to the taxes to pay their salaries. These men were called *publicans* from the fact that they were *public* servants.

This system encouraged widespread fraud and extortion, which was tolerated by the Romans and made some of the publicans very rich men. But for the Jews, these publicans were traitors to their own people and were universally hated and despised. However, while it appears that a large majority of the publicans were corrupt, there were some exceptions that we know of. The most notable was Matthew, who was a publican in the Galilee area when Jesus called him to be one of the Twelve. Though it doesn't tell us this specifically, we can assume that Matthew abandoned that comfortable life when he accepted the call of the Master. Zacchaeus, the little man who climbed up a tree to see Jesus, was another publican who was honest in his dealings with the people (see Luke 19:1–10).

Understanding the background of these two groups helps us better appreciate the short story Jesus told His listeners that day.

The two men are polar opposites. The Pharisee—supposedly a model devotee to the work of God—was filled with pride and self-aggrandizement and used his prayer as a way to let everyone know just how marvelously faithful he was, praying loudly enough for any passersby to hear. His purpose was to make sure everyone knew that he was far superior to that detestable publican praying a short distance away.

The publican, on the other hand, provided a dramatic contrast. Though he too was likely a person of wealth and influence, his demeanor was quite the opposite. Keenly aware of his spiritual failings, he wouldn't so much as look up to heaven as he prayed. Nor did he loudly enumerate the good things he had done to balance out his sins. He didn't even feel worthy enough to approach the place of prayer—the temple or synagogue—but stood afar off and hoped that his pleas would reach heaven. The contrast between the two of them could hardly be more dramatic.

Here's one more thing to consider about the Pharisee. As noted, Pharisees were the experts on the law, the masters of the scriptures, the most learned about the laws of God. They took great pride in their knowledge of the scriptures, often memorizing the entire Torah. Yet, like this one, in their pride and avarice they had forgotten the admonitions about caring for others in need that were found throughout the law of Moses. Here is but a small sampling of such directives:

- "[King] Hezekiah humbled himself for the pride of his heart, both he and the inhabitants of Jerusalem, so that the wrath of the Lord came not upon them" (2 Chronicles 32:26).
- "They cry, but none giveth answer, because of the pride of evil men" (Job 35:12).
- "The wicked in his pride doth persecute the poor: . . . The wicked, through the pride of his countenance, will not seek after God: God is not in all his thoughts" (Psalm 10:2, 4).
- "The fear of the Lord is to hate evil: pride, and arrogancy" (Proverbs 8:13).
- "When pride cometh, then cometh shame: but with the lowly is wisdom" (Proverbs 11:2).

- "Pride goeth before destruction, and an haughty spirit before a fall" (Proverbs 16:18).

- "My soul shall weep in secret places for your pride; and mine eye shall weep sore, and run down with tears, because the Lord's flock is carried away captive" (Jeremiah 13:17).

For the Pharisees there that day who were challenging Jesus's authority to teach the people, what Jesus said next must have infuriated them: "I tell you, this man [the publican] went down to his house justified rather than the other: for every one that exalteth himself shall be abased;[1] and he that humbleth himself shall be exalted" (Luke 18:14).

APPLICATION

One well-known Christian Bible scholar made these observations about this parable:

> This parable is apparently addressed . . . to certain of the disciples of Jesus who were proud *of their spiritual attainments, and lacking in the virtues of humility and penitence.*[2] . . . The words of the Pharisee can hardly be called a prayer. He asks for nothing, and feels his need of nothing. The Pharisee did, indeed, acknowledge that his virtues were derived from God, but he took all the merit of them to himself, and boasted of them before God. . . . As the Pharisee had singled himself out as the one holy [person] in the world, so the publican singles himself out as the chief of sinners, the man in whom all sins have met. (J.R. Dummelow, *The One Volume Bible Commentary*, 764–5)

Elder James E. Talmage, a member of the Quorum of the Twelve Apostles, summarized the message of the parable this way: "The parable is applicable to all men; its moral was summed up in repetition of our Lord's words spoken in the house of the chief Pharisee: 'For every one that exalteth himself shall be abased; and he that humbleth himself shall be exalted'" (*Jesus the Christ*, 472–3).

President Harold B. Lee also spoke of this parable, reminding all of us that we are called to serve in the kingdom, not to talk about how great we are in our service to others:

> I have said, and I repeat it again, the only true record that will ever be written of me will be the record that I write in the hearts of those whom I have tried to help in this world. Service brings comfort and forgiveness. Your mourning with the aged, the widow, and the orphan should lead you to bring the succor they require. In a word, you must be as the publican and not as the Pharisee. "God be merciful to me a sinner" (Luke 18:13). Your reward for so doing is the blessedness of comfort for your own soul through a forgiveness of your own sins. (*The Teachings of Harold B. Lee* [Salt Lake City: Bookcraft, 1996], 182)

CONTEXT AND SETTING: THE TWO SONS

Found only in the gospel of Matthew, here is another short parable that the Savior taught during His earthly ministry. It too carries a succinct but powerful message of gospel application.

This parable was given near the very end of Christ's mortal ministry. He had come to Jerusalem with the Twelve and others for the great Passover celebration. He would not leave Jerusalem again in His mortal state. His arrest, trial, and execution on the cross were just days away now. He clearly knew what was coming, so His teachings took on a special urgency from this point on.

The week began with Jesus making His triumphal entry into Jerusalem riding on a donkey. Some Bible scholars believe that the population of Jerusalem during Passover increased by as much as two hundred thousand people, so there were many people in the city, and many of them had come to learn more about the Man from Galilee.

When the throngs saw Him coming over the top of the Mount of Olives riding on a donkey, the sight inspired them. They took up palm fronds and waved them joyously as they followed Him along. The waving of the long and graceful palm fronds was typically used to welcome a visiting king, or other person of great importance.

The people also greeted Him with what we call the Hosanna shout, a clear sign that they saw Jesus as the promised Messiah. They joyously laid their outer cloaks and garments on the road before Him, another practice usually reserved only for visiting royalty.

Matthew records that when Jesus and the adoring multitudes entered Jerusalem, "all the city was moved, saying, Who is this? And the multitude said, This is Jesus the prophet of Nazareth of Galilee" (Matthew 21:7–11).

Once on the Temple Mount, Jesus drove out the money changers from the temple courts for the second time. Since temple contributions were a major source of wealth for the Jewish leaders, they were infuriated with Jesus, and determined to find a way to have Him killed. (That says a lot about the spirit of their so-called faith.) But they were also very aware how the people were responding to Him and didn't dare accost Him openly.

However, the triumphal entry created another problem in the eyes of the Jewish leaders. This treating of Jesus as if He were the Messiah was alarming to them. More than once in their recent history, Jewish zealots claiming to be the Messiah had risen up and tried to overthrow their conquerors. Just a few decades earlier, an insurrection broke out which eventually required the Romans to bring in more legions to quash it. Thousands of Jews were killed.

So the Romans had zero tolerance for any such threats and the

Jewish leaders knew that. If they didn't nip this so-called Messiah in the bud, they could lose everything. This was why the Jewish leaders were constantly confronting Jesus, trying to denigrate Him in the eyes of the people and deflect anything that would bring the Roman fury down upon them all.

And now, with Pilate and his legionaries in Jerusalem for the Passover, Jesus was a very real threat to their status quo. This is why when the chief priests and scribes watched the huge crowds pouring onto the Temple Mount, they immediately sought Him out to ascertain His intentions.

Speaking of the triumphal entry, they said to Jesus, *"Hearest thou what these say? And Jesus saith unto them, Yea; have ye never read, Out of the mouth of babes and sucklings thou hast perfected praise?"* (Matthew 21:16). Not only did His response trouble them, but the fact that He cited what was considered to be a Messianic prophecy alarmed them all the more.

The next day, the tension between Jesus and the Jewish leaders only intensified. Here is Matthew's account of what followed:

> And when he was come into the temple, the chief priests and the elders of the people came unto him as he was teaching, and said, By what authority doest thou these things? and who gave thee this authority? And Jesus answered and said unto them, I also will ask you one thing, which if ye tell me, I in like wise will tell you by what authority I do these things. The baptism of John [the Baptist], whence was it? from heaven, or of men?
>
> And they reasoned with themselves, saying, If we shall say, From heaven; he will say unto us, Why did ye not then believe him? But if we shall say, Of men; we fear the people; for all hold John as a prophet. And they answered Jesus, and said, We cannot tell. And he said unto them, Neither

tell I you by what authority I do these things. (Matthew 21:23–27)

Once again, Jesus had turned their question back on themselves in front of the people. It was a clever verbal trap because these Jewish leaders had publicly denied that John came with any authorization from God. How did they know that? Because he was not one of them, of course. But on this day, they were sitting in the midst of great crowds of people, most of whom strongly believed that John had come in fulfillment of prophesy as a forerunner of the Messiah. If they denied John, the crowd might rise up against them.

So, with their typical duplicity, they waffled and backed down from the confrontation. And with that response, Jesus immediately shared another parable which, like the parable of the Pharisee and the publican, was aimed directly at the corrupt Jewish leadership trying to deflect Jesus from becoming the spiritual leader of the people. This context clearly shows that Jesus was openly challenging the right of these haughty and powerful men to serve as the spiritual shepherds of the people. And He did so now, with the Passover crowds there to hear it all.

THE PARABLE

But what think ye? A certain man had two sons; and he came to the first, and said, Son, go work to day in my vineyard. He answered and said, I will not: but afterward he repented, and went. And he came to the second, and said likewise. And he answered and said, I go, sir: and went not. Whether of them twain did the will of his father? They [the Jewish leaders] say unto him, The first. Jesus saith unto them, Verily I say unto you, That the publicans and the harlots go into the kingdom of God before you.

For John came unto you in the way of righteousness, and

ye believed him not: but the publicans and the harlots believed him: and ye, when ye had seen it, repented not afterward, that ye might believe him. (Matthew 21:28–32)

ANALYSIS

This is another short parable with a message that is crystal clear in its meaning and that taught a powerful gospel principle within its brevity. It had started out with the Jewish leaders demanding to know by what authority Jesus taught the people and publicly challenged their own authority to be the spiritual leaders of the covenant people. Why? Because they were the epitome of the second son. They publicly claimed that they were the only ones who could lead the people in their faith, that they were the ones chosen by God to do His work on earth. Yet what had they done? Nothing!

There was no ambiguity in His blistering words. Jesus pointed out with perfect clarity that these pompous leaders had nothing but deep disgust for those they saw as the hopelessly wicked—i.e., the harlots and the publicans. And as the parable shows—at the same time that they professed to be going out to do the work of the Lord, they had no intention of doing it. This was the hypocrisy that Jesus so pointedly denounced.

The word *hypocrite* comes from a Greek word that described actors, or stage players in Greek drama. While on stage, they held up various masks attached to a stick in front of faces to depict the role they were playing. Thus, hypocrite suggests one who is a player, an actor, one who hides his or her true identity in order to play a part (see *Strong's Concordance*, 5271).

Hypocrite was a word that Jesus used frequently when He condemned the religious leaders of His time. Just a few days after these events on the Temple Mount, in a scathing and blistering condemnation of their values, Jesus warned the people about these false pretenders, using the word *hypocrite* over and over. He summed up their true character in these words: "Do ye not after their works: for they say, and do not" (Matthew 23:3; see all of Matthew 23).

"They say, and do not." That exactly described the second son.

The ultimate proof of the true nature of the hearts of these rich and powerful men was that before the week was out, they would be the ones who were screaming at Pilate, who had found no fault in Jesus, "Crucify him! Crucify him!" (Luke 23:21).

Elder James E. Talmage wrote of this parable and suggested that it was a metaphor for any or all that are invited to come into the covenant and become the children of God. Some initially reject the missionaries and turn away, but later have a change of heart and enter the "vineyard" to work. He suggests that this simple story has application for all who are called to the work.

Although this excellent parable was addressed to the chief priests, scribes, and elders, who had come in hostile spirit to demand of Christ the credentials of His authority, *its lesson is of universal application.* The two sons are yet alive in every human community—the one openly boastful of his sin, the other a hypocritical pretender. Jesus did not commend the rough refusal of the first son of whom the father made a righteous demand for service; it was his subsequent repentance attended by works that made him superior to his brother who had made fair promise but had kept it not. There are many today who boast that they make no profession of religion, nor pretense of godly life. Their frankness will not mitigate their sins; it simply shows that a certain species of hypocrisy is not prominent among their numerous offenses; but that a man is innocent of one vice, say that of drunkenness, in no wise diminishes his measure of guilt if he be a liar, a thief, an adulterer, or a murderer. Both the sons in the parable were grievous sinners; but the one turned from his evil ways, which theretofore he had followed with flagrant openness, while the other continued in dark deeds of sin, which he sought to cover by a cloak of hypocrisy. (*Jesus the Christ,* 541)

We close this discussion of the two sons in the parable with the words of the Savior given early in His ministry on a mount near the Sea of Galilee. It is the doctrine that the Jewish leaders had abandoned:

Beware of false prophets, which come to you in sheep's clothing, but inwardly they are ravening wolves. Ye shall know them by their fruits. Do men gather grapes of thorns, or figs of thistles? Even so every good tree bringeth forth good fruit; but a corrupt tree bringeth forth evil fruit. A good tree cannot bring forth evil fruit, neither can a corrupt tree bring forth good fruit. Every tree that bringeth not forth good fruit is hewn down, and cast into the fire. Wherefore by their fruits [not just their words] ye shall know them.

Not every one that saith unto me, Lord, Lord, shall enter into the kingdom of heaven; but he that doeth the will of my Father which is in heaven. Many will say to me in that day, Lord, Lord, have we not prophesied in thy name? and in thy name have cast out devils? and in thy name done many wonderful works? And then will I profess unto them, I never knew you3: depart from me, ye that work iniquity.

Therefore whosoever heareth these sayings of mine, and doeth them, I will liken him unto a wise man, which built his house upon a rock: And the rain descended, and the floods came, and the winds blew, and beat upon that house;

and it fell not: for it was founded upon a rock. And every one that heareth these sayings of mine, and doeth them not, shall be likened unto a foolish man, which built his house upon the sand: And the rain descended, and the floods came, and the winds blew, and beat upon that house; and it fell: and great was the fall of it. (Matthew 7:15–27)

In conclusion, in my teens, I was introduced to a short poem by my father that summarizes the central importance of the choices we make and how those choices shape what we become. Two verses from that poem have application here:

Princes and Kings

Isn't it strange how princes and kings,
and clowns that caper in sawdust rings,
and common people, like you and me,
are builders of eternity?

Each is given a list of rules;
a shapeless mass, a bag of tools.
And each must fashion, ere life is flown,
a stumbling block or a stepping stone.

—R. Lee Sharpe

NOTES

1. Abased: "To make low, bring low . . . bring to a humble position" (*Strong's Concordance*, 5011).
2. That is a good reminder that this parable has relevance to His disciples in our day as well.
3. The JST changes this to "You never *knew me*" (JST Matthew 7).

Part III

Ministering

Chapter 8

Jesus Formally Opens His Mortal Ministry

Before we examine the parables in this section of the book, which focus on ministering, it will be enlightening to see how the Savior viewed ministering as it related to His own mission here in mortality.

Luke, who has much that is unique to his gospel record, included several aspects of Jesus's life before His formal ministry began. These include:

- The angel Gabriel's visit to Zacharias while officiating in the temple to announce that his wife, Elisabeth, who was barren, would bring forth a son they would name John, who would be the forerunner of the Messiah (see Luke 1:5–25).

- The visit of Gabriel to Mary in Nazareth with the stunning news that she would conceive a child who would be the Son of God and redeem all mankind (see Luke 1:26–38).

- Mary's visit to Elisabeth and the birth of John the Baptist (see Luke 1:39–56).

- The birth of John the Baptist (see Luke 1:57–80).

- The Nativity story and Joseph and Mary's experience in the temple after the birth of Christ (see Luke 2:1–39).

- A brief glimpse into the childhood of Jesus, including His visit to Jerusalem at age twelve, where He taught the Jewish elders (see Luke 2:40–52). Though Luke does not tell us how he received such intimate and personal details about Jesus and His family, these recorded details have been treasured for many generations.

There is another account Luke includes in his record that is also unique and that gives us an insight into the Savior's life that is of great significance, but it is often passed over as being a nice insight but not of much doctrinal importance. However, a careful look at the passage suggests that Luke may have included it in his record because it provides a unique declaration of the Savior's mission during His sojourn in mortality, given by the Savior Himself. Luke records this immediately following the forty days of temptation in the wilderness and the beginning of Jesus's ministry.

Though it is not directly connected to the parables in this section, what happened in Nazareth one Sabbath day seems to have signaled the formal beginning of His mortal ministry. And what is of special interest in this study is that the passage from Isaiah that Jesus chose to cite that day (see Isaiah 61:1–3) defined in specific detail what Jesus saw His ministry should be during His mortal sojourn on earth.

IN THE SYNAGOGUE AT NAZARETH

To understand this passage, it is helpful to understand something about the customary Jewish worship in the synagogues of that time. Each Sabbath day, as part of the worship service, there was a time when the scrolls that held the sacred scriptures—mostly what we now know as the Old Testament—were opened and read aloud to the congregation. Any worthy adult male member, including boys age twelve and older, could come up and read from the scrolls. This was considered to be an especially sacred time, and great solemnity was expected of all who were in attendance that day.

The person would stand up and read from the sacred writings. It is not clear if the individual could select a passage of his choice, if the leader of the synagogue chose a passage, or if they read through the scriptures in a sequential manner and the reader picked up where the last person had left off.

Remember, this was the village where Jesus had grown up. He now was about thirty years old. Though Luke doesn't mention this, He was likely there with His mother and other family members, because Nazareth was His hometown. There is no mention of Joseph after the accounts of their visit to Jerusalem when Jesus was twelve, and some scholars assume that Joseph was dead by that time. But that is only speculation.

As the scroll was brought out, Jesus came forward, indicating that He would like to be the one to read. He was presented with a scroll that included the writings of Isaiah. Though the leader of the synagogue might give the reader a specific passage to read, as noted, it's possible the reader chose a passage, and that could be what Jesus did that day.

Luke then recorded: "And when he had opened the book, he found the place where it was written. . . ." (Luke 4:17). Jesus then read two passages from what we now call the book of Isaiah. The first comes from Isaiah 61:1–2, and the second from Isaiah 42:7:

> The Spirit of the Lord is upon me, because he hath anointed me to preach the gospel to the poor; he hath sent me to heal the broken hearted; to preach deliverance to the captives; and recovering sight to the blind, to set at liberty them that are bruised, to preach the acceptable year of the Lord. And he closed the book, and he gave it again to the minister, and sat down. (Luke 4:18–20)

When He finished, Jesus added a declaration of His own. He said: "This day is this scripture fulfilled in your ears" (Luke 4:21). In other words, the ancient prophecy of Isaiah, given more than seven hundred years earlier, was now at hand.

That declaration must have had a stunning effect on the people, for this passage from Isaiah was considered to be prophecy of the long-foretold coming of the Messiah. Was Jesus actually telling them that He was the living fulfillment of that prophecy? It certainly seems so based on how the people reacted. Some in the congregation were shocked and asked each other, "Is not this Joseph's son?" (Luke 4:22). In other words, "Is this boy that we watched grow up actually claiming that He is the Messiah?"

Overhearing that, Jesus's response was a gentle rebuke: "Verily, I say unto you, No prophet is accepted in His own country" (Luke 4:24).

For a person to claim that he was the Messiah was considered both blasphemy and heresy. In the Mosaic law, these acts were punishable by death. Luke then tells us that "they [most likely the rulers and elders of the synagogue] rose up, and thrust him out of the city, and led him unto the brow of the hill whereon their city was built, that they might cast him down headlong. But he passing through the midst of them went his way" (Luke 4:28–30).

A short distance south of the town of Nazareth there is a precipice that drops off sharply from its crest. This is the likely place where they took Him with the intent to throw Him off and kill the blasphemer. But this was not His time to die. Somehow He escaped their grasp and left the village. There is no record that He ever returned to His childhood home.

However, our focus here is not so much on *what* He did that day but on the passage He selected to define His purpose for coming to earth. And that purpose can be summed up with one word: He came to *minister!*

In the New Testament, the word translated in English as *minister* means to render service; to help others; to help sustain life; to supply necessities to others; to take care of the poor and the sick; to attend to anything that might serve the interests of others (see *Strong's Concordance*, 1247). And while Isaiah did not use the word *minister*, each one of his list of items describes a way that we can minister to others. Thus, by citing this passage from Isaiah, Jesus made a very clear declaration that His calling was to minister, and that His formal ministry had now begun.

Three years later, as He and His followers went to Jerusalem for Passover for the last time, Jesus knew it was time to pass on the keys and authority He held to those who would take up the work from this point on. At Nazareth, He had confirmed that He had come to minister. At Jerusalem, shortly before His death, Jesus formally gave the Twelve a charge to do the same.

> Jesus called them unto him, and said, Ye know that the princes of the Gentiles exercise dominion over them, and they that are great exercise authority upon them. But it shall not be so among you: but whosoever will be great among you, let him be your minister; And whosoever will be chief among you, let him be your servant: Even as the Son of man came not to be ministered unto, but to minister, and to give his life a ransom for many. (Matthew 20:25–28)

When Jesus called twelve men to be His Apostles, He charged them go forth preaching that "the kingdom of heaven is at hand. Heal the sick, cleanse the lepers, raise the dead, cast out devils; freely ye have received, freely give" (Matthew 10:7–8).

Luke tells us that He gave a similar but more extensive directive when He called seventy men, and "sent them two and two before his face into every city and place" (Luke 10:1; see also verses 2–16). Luke then records: "And the seventy returned again with joy, saying, Lord, even the devils are subject unto us through thy name" (Luke 10:17). Clearly, ministering to those in need was a central part of the Savior's mortal mission. Therefore, it should not surprise us that He admonishes His followers then and today to minister to the needs of others.

And with that brief lesson on the role of ministering in the kingdom, we turn to examine the parables of Jesus Christ that have a particular focus on how, when, where, and to whom we are called to minister as the Savior ministered.

Chapter 9

The Good Samaritan

This parable—which some would describe as the most well-known and beloved of all the parables—is another literary jewel. It is found only in Luke's gospel. In the beginning of Luke 10, we are told that Jesus had called seventy men and sent them out two-by-two as missionaries to teach the gospel. Some time later, the seventy returned with joy and announced that even the devils were subject unto them (see Luke 10:17).

Luke reported that Jesus "rejoiced in spirit" at this time (Luke 10:21) and privately told His disciples that they were blessed to see all of these things happen.

What immediately follows in Luke's record was an incident that led Jesus to give the parable of the good Samaritan. A lawyer[1] who had come to hear Jesus teach asked Him this question: "What shall I do to inherit eternal life?" (Luke 10:25).

This was a question the rabbis loved to debate in their schools. Sometimes they expressed that more explicitly as, "Which of all the commandments is the most important for me to keep if I am to have eternal life?"

Jesus turned the question right back on the seeker. "What is written in the law? How readest thou?" (Luke 10:26). He was a lawyer, supposedly an expert in the Mosaic law. So what did he think?

The lawyer immediately answered, citing scriptures from the Old Testament: "Thou shalt love the Lord thy God with all thy heart, and with all thy soul, and with all thy strength, and with all thy mind; and thy neighbor as thyself" (Luke 10:27; see also Deuteronomy 6:4–5; Leviticus 19:18). To which the Savior said, "Thou hast answered right: this do, and thou shalt live" (Luke 10:28).

Not satisfied with that, the lawyer asked another question: "And who is my neighbour?" (Luke 10:29).

When we think about it, this last question is quite revealing about the lawyer's character. By asking who his neighbor was, he was asking, "So who do I have to love?" Which also comes with a flip side. "Who can I *not* love and still be acceptable to God?"

Jesus's answer was the story of the good Samaritan.

THE PARABLE

And Jesus answering said, A certain man went down from Jerusalem to Jericho, and fell among thieves, which stripped him of his raiment, and wounded him, and departed, leaving him half dead.

And by chance there came down a certain priest that way: and when he saw him, he passed by on the other side. And likewise a Levite, when he was at the place, came and looked on him, and passed by on the other side.

But a certain Samaritan, as he journeyed, came where he was: and when he saw him, he had compassion on him, And went to him, and bound up his wounds, pouring in oil and wine, and set him on his own beast, and brought him to an inn, and took care of him. And on the morrow when he departed, he took out two pence,[2] and gave them to the host, and said unto him, Take care of him; and whatsoever thou spendest more, when I come again, I will repay thee. (Luke 10:30–35)

That ends the formal parable, but not Jesus's teaching of the law-yer who had asked the question. He asked the lawyer His own question. "Which now of these three, thinkest thou, was neighbour unto him that fell among the thieves? And he said, He that shewed mercy on him. Then said Jesus unto him, Go, and do thou likewise" (Luke 10:36–37).

ANALYSIS

The first thing to note is that this parable does not have quite the same parallel structure found in other parables. Some experts have wondered if this was a true story and not a parable because it is more of a narrative than other parables. We don't know the answer to that, but here is something else to consider: When Jesus taught these parables, He was speaking to people of the same culture as He was; who lived in the same area that He did; who spoke the same language as He did; who knew the same history as He did; and who, for the most part, held to the same religious beliefs as He did.

We modern readers come from a very different time, a very different culture, a very different religion, and most of us do not know many details of their history. And in this case, knowing more about the key individuals in this story helps us more fully understand the impact of what Jesus taught that day.

First, the setting. Jesus described the road from Jerusalem to Jericho as going "down." That general description understates the actual area. The city of Jerusalem is nestled on top of a mountain ridge that runs through the central part of the Holy Land. The Mediterranean Sea is about twenty or so miles to the west, and the Dead Sea about the same distance to the east. That ridge is about 2,500 feet above sea level. Jericho, on the other hand, sits in the

Jordan Valley near the north end of the Dead Sea, which is the low-est spot on the face of our planet. Jericho has an elevation of about 850 feet below sea level. The distance from Jerusalem to Jericho is only about fifteen miles, which means that road drops over three thousand feet in only fifteen miles!

Anciently, the road led through a series of deep, narrow wadis, or canyons, that cut their way through the Judean wilderness. Even today, much of it is a barren, isolated, and uninhabited wilderness where only a few widely scattered Bedouin families herd their sheep and goats.

This topography and its isolation made a perfect place for rob-bers and brigands to lie in wait and attack isolated travelers. Because of this danger, people usually did not travel the road alone. So to hear of a traveler alone on that road would have been shocking to the Savior's listeners.

Jesus tells us nothing about the ethnicity of the traveler. But the setting and the story suggest that he was most likely a Jew and a resident of Jerusalem, since he was coming from there. His ethnicity is important for reasons to be explained in a moment.

In the parable, Jesus tells of three other men who were traveling the road and who came upon the victim of this assault. One was a *priest*. One was a *Levite*. One was a *Samaritan*. Knowing more about these individuals helps us better appreciate the powerful message of this narrative.

Levite: A Levite was a direct descendant of the tribe of Levi. Back in the time of Moses, God gave Levi and his male descendants the responsibility of the maintenance and daily care of the tabernacle of Moses and all of the ordinances associated with it. Their calling was to provide both the temporal and spiritual support required by the law of Moses, such as shepherding the flocks destined for sacrifice in the temple, cutting the wood for the fires used in the sacrifices, purifying the sacred olive oil used to light the lamps at night, and so on. This Levitical service continued after a permanent temple was constructed by Solomon and was still required of them in Jesus's day.

Priest: The priests were also descended from the tribe of Levi, but through the lineage of Aaron, the brother of Moses. The Lord gave Aaron and his worthy male descendants the responsibility for the *most sacred of the rites and ceremonies* of the law of Moses, including the offering of sacrifices and other sacred rituals. The Levites prepared those things, but the priests were the ones who ministered these ordinances to the people. Because of that, they were held to a higher expectation of worthiness than the Levites. Both were expected to be faithful spiritual models, but the priests especially so. Both, by their very callings, would be obligated to stop and help anyone in need.

To report that a Levite *and* a priest had ignored their responsibility for caring for those in need would have shocked most people of the day. Here is how one author described it:

> Priest and Levite are mentioned here, partly because they were the most frequent travelers on the road[3], and partly to show that these were the persons who, from the nature of their office, were most obliged to perform works of mercy; and from whom a person in distress *had a right to expect immediate succour and comfort*; and their inhuman conduct here was a flat breach of the law [of Moses]. (Adam Clarke, *Clarke's Commentary*, 3:433)

The Samaritan: After the death of King Solomon (about 975 BC), his son ascended to the throne and threatened to make things very harsh for his subjects. Civil war erupted in Israel and the tribes split into two kingdoms. Ten of the tribes stayed loyal to the new king and formed the Kingdom of Israel, or the Northern

Kingdom. Its capital was Samaria. Eventually, its citizens were called Samaritans.

The two most southern tribes—Judah and most of Benjamin— revolted and created the Kingdom of Judah, or the Southern Kingdom. Its capital was Jerusalem.

As noted in an earlier chapter, in 721 BC, the Assyrian Empire took the Northern Kingdom into captivity and they disappeared to history. The few survivors left behind were of the poorest classes.

As was customary, the Assyrians left garrisons of troops behind to protect the new territory from other predators. Over the years, these residents intermarried with their occupiers and the Samaritans became people of mixed blood. Later their descendants claimed that they had kept their religion from dying out and wanted to be included with the Jews in the Southern Kingdom. But the Jews saw them as heathens, a people of a corrupted religion, and they totally shunned them. Over the following centuries, a deep hatred and animosity developed between the Jews and the Samaritans. By the time of Jesus, this hostility was deeply rooted in both groups. It ran so deep that many of the Jews believed that to even set foot on Samaritan soil was spiritually contaminating and required a ritual cleansing.

Incidentally, Jesus ignored such traditions and traveled back and forth through Samaria more than once. It was in Samaria that He had the interchange with the woman at the well (see John 4). She was deeply shocked that a Jew would even speak to her. And when the Samaritans refused to give Jesus and the disciples lodging for the night, James and John were so incensed at this snub, they asked Jesus to call down fire on the town and totally destroy it (see Luke 9:51–56). These examples help us better understand the significance of this being a Samaritan who stopped to help the victim when the spiritual elite of Judaism had refused to do so.

What is most astounding about the Samaritan is that he didn't just stop to see if the man was still alive. Keep in mind that the Samaritan is also alone out there on that desolate and dangerous stretch of road. Even stopping for a moment put him in immediate danger. But that did not deter him from having compassion on the man. Note how Jesus described the Samaritan's efforts:

- He went to him.
- He bound up his wounds, pouring in oil and wine (to disinfect and help heal the wounds).
- He set him on his own beast, likely a donkey.
- He took him to an inn (which could have been miles away).
- He stayed overnight at the inn and cared for him.
- Though he had to continue on his own journey the next day, he paid the innkeeper the costs accrued, charged him to care for the victim until he was better, and promised to pay him more if needed when he came back that way again. Talk about going the extra mile. That would have been astounding for a Jew. But for a Samaritan to do that for a Jew? *Incredible!*

We don't know if this lawyer had heard Jesus preach before that "all things whatsoever ye would that men should do to you, do ye even so to them" (Matthew 7:12). But that was exactly what the Samaritan had done for the victim.

APPLICATION

With that background, we can better appreciate what immediately followed. Jesus now turned back to the lawyer, who very likely was reeling a little from what he had just heard. This was the same man who had asked Jesus, "Who is my neighbor?" or in other words, "Who am I required to love?" Now Jesus asked him to answer his own question: "Which now of these three, thinkest thou, was neighbour unto him that fell among the thieves?" (Luke 10:36).

It must have been a painful question for the lawyer, for there was obviously only one answer to that, and he knew it. "And he said, He that shewed mercy on him" (Luke 10:37).

In one of those tiny details we find in the parables that reveal so much about people's character, note that the lawyer did not answer with, "The Samaritan." It's as if even saying that word was so painful to him that he couldn't bring himself to do it. So instead he described his actions. "He that shewed mercy."

Jesus found that answer acceptable: "Then said Jesus unto him, Go, and do thou likewise" (Luke 10:37).

In this simple but powerful parable, we are introduced to five typical attitudes often found in human nature that determine how we interact with those in need.

The injured victim: "I am in need. Help me!"

The thieves: "What's yours is ours if we are strong enough to take it."

The priest and Levite: "What's mine is mine and I'm going to keep it."

The innkeeper: "What's mine is yours if you can pay for it."

The Samaritan: "What's mine is yours if you need it."

At the synagogue in Nazareth, Jesus defined one of the things that He had come to earth to do. He came to minister to others. We note the list again (see Luke 4:18–19):

- Preach the gospel to the poor.
- Heal the brokenhearted.
- Preach deliverance to the captives.
- Give sight to the blind.
- Set at liberty them that are bruised.
- Preach the acceptable year of the Lord.

Put very simply, while His primary purpose in coming to earth was to make an infinite Atonement for all of God's children and give them the opportunity to return to the presence of our Heavenly Father, He also came to set a perfect example for us on how to live so that we could do that. And a major part of that "how to live" counsel was learning to minister to others. The Savior set the standard for all of us when He asked, "Therefore, what manner of men ought ye to be?" The answer was simple and unmistakably clear: "Verily I say unto you, even as I am" (3 Nephi 27:27).

And in the parable of the good Samaritan, He gives us a model of how to do that.

Our modern prophets, seers, and revelators have echoed that charge: President Gordon B. Hinckley summed up the lesson of this parable with this simple reminder: "There are so many who have been injured and who need a Good Samaritan to bind up their wounds and help them on their way. A small kindness can bring a great blessing to someone in distress and a sweet feeling to the one who befriends him" (*Teachings,* 287).

President M. Russell Ballard focused on the Savior's words to the lawyer to "Go and do," and added these insights.:

> Our latter-day prophets are well known for such phrases as "Let's get going," "Do it," "Do it now." I have heard President Gordon B. Hinckley say that the only way he knows to get things done is to first get on his knees and pray, and then to get on his feet and go do the work. That driving desire to "go" and "do" has been the hallmark of our prophet-presidents all of their lives. Of course, "going and doing" isn't always easy or comfortable. Occasionally it requires some sacrifice on our part—of time, energy, or personal will. But it is almost always worth whatever effort we make, especially if it has to do with following the instructions of

inspired council leaders in seeking to bring souls to Christ. (*Counseling with our Councils,* 32)

In recent years, the concept of ministering has taken on new relevance for members of The Church of Jesus Christ of Latter-day Saints. In the general conference where President Russell M. Nelson was sustained as our seventeenth prophet, seer, and revelator and President of the Church, he announced a change of emphasis in how we serve each other in the kingdom of God. As part of that, he introduced a new approach in the Church simply called "ministering," which he called "a new and holier way." In the priesthood session of that conference he said:

A hallmark of the Lord's true and living Church will always be an organized, directed effort to minister to individual children of God and their families. Because it is His Church, we as His servants will minister to the one, just as He did. We will minister in His name, with His power and authority, and with His loving-kindness. ("Ministering with the Power and Authority of God," *Ensign,* May 2018)

He then announced a change from the home and visiting teaching programs to ministering to those in need. He made it clear that this change would permeate all levels of Church service and be part of the work of all of the organizations of the Church.

By the time this book is published, that change to a focus on ministering to others will be about five years old. As we ponder on this marvelous parable, this would be a good time to ask ourselves a lot of questions about how we are doing in our ministering callings. But let's use the Savior as our model and ask ourselves the question that He asked the lawyer that day: "Which now of these three, thinkest thou, was neighbour unto him that fell among the thieves?

And he said, He that shewed mercy on him. Then said Jesus unto him, Go, and do thou likewise" (Luke 10:36–37).

Sister Sharon Eubank, First Counselor in the Relief Society General Presidency, cited a talk given by the Prophet Joseph Smith to a group of sisters in Nauvoo in 1842 where he spoke of the need for love and kindness in the gospel. His words strongly support what Jesus taught in the parable of the good Samaritan. She quoted much of it. Here is what the Prophet Joseph taught the women that day—and all of us today:

> Nothing is so much calculated to lead people to forsake sin as to take them by the hand and watch over them with tenderness. When persons manifest the least kindness and love to me, O what pow'r it has over my mind, while the opposite course has a tendency to harrow up all the harsh feelings and depress the human mind. It is one evidence that men are unacquainted with the principle of godliness, to behold the contraction of feeling and lack of charity. The pow'r and glory of godliness is spread out on a broad principle to throw out the mantle of charity. God does not look on sin with allowance, but when men have sin'd there must be allowance made for them.
>
> All the religious world is boasting of its righteousness—it is the doctrine of the devil to retard the human mind and retard our progress by filling us with self righteousness—The nearer we get to our heavenly Father the more are we disposed to look with compassion on perishing souls to take them upon our shoulders and cast their sins behind our back. I am going to talk to all this Society—if you would have God have mercy on you, have mercy on one another. ("Minutes and Discourse, 9 June 1842," 62,

Joseph Smith Papers, josephsmithpapers.org/paper-summary
/minutes-and-discourse-9-june-1842/2)

In summary: What the Savior taught us in this remarkable parable is that it is not enough for us to ask, "*Who* do I need to love?" We also need to ask ourselves, "*How* do I need to love?"

NOTES

1. This is almost certainly one of the scribes and not a lawyer as we know them today. The scribes are often mentioned in connection with the Pharisees, and many of them were Pharisees. The scribes could both read and write and were experts in the intricacies and complexities of the law of Moses, which was both the civil and religious law at that time.
2. Roughly $300 in today's currency.
3. Jericho was known as a city where many of the priests and Levites lived, which meant that they often traveled between there and Jerusalem.

Chapter 10

The Lost Sheep;
The Lost Coin

We shall examine three parables about lost things at this point in our study. Each one reflects different aspects of being lost. Each one also teaches how these lost things can be found again. They are the parable of the lost sheep, the parable of the lost coin, and the parable of the prodigal son.

Since all three parables follow one after the other without any additional commentary from the Savior, we shall use the same context and setting for all three here. In this chapter we shall examine the first two, which are both very short. The parable of the prodigal son is much longer and more complex, so we shall discuss that in the next chapter.

CONTEXT AND SETTING

The lost sheep, the first of these parables, is found in both the gospel of Matthew and the gospel of Luke, with very little variation between the two accounts. However, the context and setting where Matthew places it (see Matthew 18:11–14) is significantly different from Luke's setting (see Luke 15:1–7). This may be because Jesus taught this parable more than once.

Matthew records that some of the disciples of Jesus came to Him and asked Him who was the greatest in the kingdom of heaven. He used the innocence of little children as the model for entry into that kingdom and warned them about offending these innocents. He then spoke of the lost sheep. Matthew did not speak of other lost things in his account (see Matthew 18:1–14).

In Luke's gospel, Jesus was teaching among the people when there "drew near unto him all the publicans and sinners for to hear him. And the Pharisees and scribes murmured, saying, This man receive sinners, and eateth with them" (Luke 15:1–2). In their minds, the common people, and especially anyone who did not accept them as the spiritual elites of their day, were sinners and were to be avoided, especially in social settings such as sharing a meal together.

We learned about "the publicans," or tax collectors, in a previous chapter, and how they were detested by the high-minded scribes and Pharisees. "Sinners" was the scornful name the Jewish religious leaders, and especially the Pharisees, gave to anyone and everyone who didn't accept them as the final authority in spiritual matters. As a group, the scribes and the Pharisees firmly believed that they were the *only* ones who would be chosen to enter the kingdom of heaven. The aristocratic and haughty Sadducees didn't believe in the Resurrection and life after death at all, which seems especially odd for religious leaders of the covenant people. They lived lives of high privilege and great luxury, and they were willing to do just about anything to protect their status.

Since it is in Luke that we find all three parables of lost things placed one right after another—the lost sheep, the lost coin, and the prodigal son—we shall study his record and look at them one by one.

THE PARABLE: THE LOST SHEEP

What man of you, having an hundred sheep, if he lose one of them, doth not leave the ninety and nine in the wilderness,[1] and go after that which is lost, until he find it? And when he hath found it, he layeth it on his shoulders, rejoicing. And when he cometh home, he calleth together his friends and neighbours, saying unto them, Rejoice with me; for I have found my sheep which was lost. I say unto you, that likewise joy shall be in heaven over one sinner that repenteth, more than over ninety and nine just persons, which need no repentance. (Luke 15:4–7)

ANALYSIS AND APPLICATION

In our day, if we are out in the countryside, we may sometimes see huge flocks of sheep—sometimes five thousand or more—that are watched over by hired sheepherders with horses or ATVs, sheep dogs, short wave radios, and enclosed heated trailers with indoor stoves and refrigerators. In most cases, these modern shepherds drive their flocks from behind with the help of their horses, ATVs, and dogs.

But in the Middle East in the time of Jesus, and even today, the role of the nomadic shepherd is very different, and so are the ways they care for their flocks.

George M. Mackie, a Christian minister for the Church of Scotland (1854–1922), lived for twenty years in Lebanon serving as a pastor for his church. He later wrote a book on his experiences there, focusing on how aspects of the culture he saw there were still much the same as they were in the time of Jesus. His book *Bible Manners and Customs* provides rich insight into the culture and habits in the time of Christ. One of those things he described was the shepherd and his flock:

By day and by night the shepherd is always with his sheep. . . . He depends on the sheep to follow, and they in turn expect him never to leave them. They run after him if he appears to be escaping from them, and are terrified when he is out of sight, or any stranger appears instead of him. He calls to them from time to time to let them know that he is at hand. The sheep listen and continue grazing, but if any one else tries to produce the same peculiar cries and guttural sounds, they look around with a startled air and begin to scatter. . . . As he is always with them, . . . the shepherd comes to know his sheep very intimately. . . .

At sunset the sheep are counted, usually two by two; but as a rule when they are brought together the absence of any one is immediately *felt*. One day a missionary meeting a shepherd on one of the wildest parts of Lebanon, asked him various questions about his sheep, and among other things if he counted them every night. On answering that he did not, he was asked how he knew if they were all there or not. His reply was: "Master, if you were to put a cloth over my eyes, and bring me any sheep and only let me put my hands on its face, I could tell in a moment if it was mine or not." (*Bible Manners and Customs*, 33–35)

Jesus described Himself as "the good shepherd," using imagery similar to Mackie's description (see John 10:1–15). He concluded with this declaration: "I am the good shepherd, and *know my sheep, and am known of mine*" (John 10:14; emphasis added).

The shepherd's care for the sheep is the main point of the parable. The lost sheep was only one of a large flock, and some might say that the loss wasn't that critical. But not so for the shepherd! Though the search would likely involve considerable effort, loss of time, and possible danger, the shepherd set out immediately. There was no question in his mind about just writing it off as the natural risks of herding. And many of his friends and family felt the same, for there was a joyous celebration among the shepherd's family and friends when he returned with his sheep.

President Dieter F. Uchtdorf made an interesting observation about the parable of the lost sheep:

> Over the centuries, this parable has traditionally been interpreted as a call to action for us to bring back the lost sheep and to reach out to those who are lost. While this is certainly appropriate and good, I wonder if there is more to it. Is it possible that Jesus's purpose, first and foremost, was to teach about the work of the Good Shepherd? Is it possible that He was testifying of God's love for His wayward children?
>
> Is it possible that the Savior's message was that God is fully aware of those who are lost—and that He will find them, that He will reach out to them, and that He will rescue them? If that is so, what must the sheep do to qualify for this divine help? Does the sheep need to know how to use a complicated sextant to calculate its coordinates? Does it need to be able to use a GPS to define its position? Does it have to have the expertise to create an app that will call for help? Does the sheep need endorsements by a sponsor before the Good Shepherd will come to the rescue?
>
> No. Certainly not! The sheep is worthy of divine rescue simply because it is loved by the Good Shepherd. To me, the parable of the lost sheep is one of the most hopeful passages in all of scripture. ("He Will Place You On His Shoulders and Carry You Home," *Ensign*, May 2016)

THE PARABLE: THE LOST COIN

Either what woman having ten pieces of silver, if she lose one piece, doth not light a candle, and sweep the house, and seek diligently till she find it. And when she hath found it, she calleth her friends and her neighbours together, saying, Rejoice with me; for I have found the piece which I had lost. (Luke 15:8–9)

ANALYSIS AND APPLICATION

Luke describes the lost money as being one of "ten pieces of silver." The Greek word used here is *drachma*, which was a coin similar to and worth about the same amount as the Roman *denarius* described earlier in the parable of the laborers in the vineyard. For those of the working classes, one drachma was a significant amount of money, well over a hundred dollars in our day. Though we don't have exact equivalents, it appears that one piece of silver would be about as valuable to the woman as one sheep would have been to the shepherd.

These two parables are so similar in nature that one might be tempted to link them together into one parable with two examples. But there are some differences.

The primary difference is that the sheep was a living thing. The coin was not. There are other differences as well. The coin, being an inanimate object, was most likely lost through carelessness. The sheep wandered off on its own. When it comes to people, we lose some in both ways.

The parables also have their similarities. In each, the owner showed deep concern for the lost item and made diligent efforts to recover it. In other words, it didn't matter *how* each item was lost. The effort to recover it and the joy when it was recovered were very much the same.

Consider also the question that triggered Matthew's account of the lost sheep. Someone asked the Savior, "Who will enter into the kingdom of heaven?" The flip side of that question is, "Who will *not* get into the kingdom of heaven?" The initial response seems to be, "Those that are lost." But the lesson of each of these two parables would answer that question with four additional words: "Those that are lost *and are not found.*"

Elder Jeffrey R. Holland bore his witness of the goodness and long-suffering of God, which is taught in these parables of the lost, citing something the Prophet Joseph Smith taught in his day:

> I bear personal witness this day of a personal, living God, who knows our names, hears and answers prayers, and cherishes us eternally as children of His spirit. I testify that amidst the wondrously complex tasks inherent in the universe, He seeks our individual happiness and safety above all other godly concerns. ("The Grandeur of God," *Ensign*, November 2003)

The Prophet Joseph Smith also described the mercy and love of God for His children:

> Our heavenly Father is more liberal in His views, and boundless in His mercies and blessings, than we are ready to believe or receive. . . . God does not look on sin with [the least degree of] allowance, but . . . *the nearer we get to our heavenly Father, the more we are disposed to look with compassion on perishing souls; we feel that we want to take them upon our shoulders, and cast their sins behind our backs.* (In Joseph Fielding Smith, *Teachings of the Prophet Joseph Smith*, 240–41; emphasis added)

How far from that sentiment were the scribes and Pharisees of Jesus's day!

NOTES

1. Joseph Smith corrected this verse to say that the shepherd left the flock in a safe place and it was he who went into the wilderness to find the lost one (see JST, Luke 15:4). This is much more in line with what the shepherds of old would have done.

Chapter 11

The Prodigal Son

CONTEXT AND SETTING

As noted in the previous chapter, after the scribes and the Pharisees complained about Jesus mingling with what they called "sinners" (see Luke 15:2), Jesus answered them with three parables given one right after the other—the lost sheep, the lost coin, and the prodigal son. Each parable gives us an example from real life of lost "things." So in one way, the context and setting is the same for this third parable as it was for the first two.

But this parable is very different in several ways. In the first place, those first parables were very short—together they took only six verses. Here, the full story of the prodigal son is more than three times that much.

Another difference is that the first two parables were about lost things whereas this one is about lost souls. We say "souls" because in a way, as we shall see, we have two lost sons here, not just one. The sullen and resentful older brother, who, in his own way, was as disdainful about his younger brother as were the scribes and the Pharisees about those they called "wicked."

This account of the family has so much detail in it that some scholars have wondered if it might have been based on actual happenings Jesus knew of. There is no way to know that for sure, but either way, the parable teaches some important principles about ministering to others as the Savior did in His life.

Though this parable is more complex than the first two parables, it too teaches us some principles about recovering "lost things." And, as we have seen with other parables, here too we have an example of a literary masterpiece as the Savior vividly describes the primary players in this story.

Though we find in this parable some aspects of the parallel, parabolic structure that are common to other parables of Jesus, due to its narrative form, we shall not examine them in the side-by-side format. Also, due to its length, we shall break the parable and our analysis of it into smaller portions so that it is easier to follow the flow of this literary jewel. We shall also combine the analysis and application sections together since they are so closely linked.

THE PARABLE

And he [Jesus] said, A certain man had two sons: And the younger of them said to his father, Father, give me the portion of goods that falleth to me. And he divided unto them his living. And not many days after the younger son gathered all together, and took his journey into a far country, and there wasted his substance with riotous living). (Luke 15: 11-13)

And when he had spent all, there arose a mighty famine in that land; and he began to be in want. And he went and joined himself to a citizen of that country; and he sent him into his fields to feed swine. And he would fain have filled his belly with the husks that the swine did eat: and no man gave unto him. (Luke 15:11–16)

ANALYSIS AND APPLICATION

From a literary standpoint, note how much detail Jesus conveyed about this young man in such a few words:

- "Not many days after." Once the decision was made to give him his inheritance, the young man was eager to leave, break his ties with the family, and launch into his new life.

- He "gathered all together." This is more than packing for an extended vacation. This young man had no plans to return in the foreseeable future. In his mind this was a permanent separation, or at least for a very long time.

- He went to a "far country." Of course he did! When we choose to sever our ties with our family and start anew, who wants to be just a few miles away? Breaking what are viewed as the shackles and achieving one's independence appears to be one of the powerful motivators pushing him to leave his family. A "far country" suggests distance *and* long-term separation. The son seems to be hoping for a life where he will no longer be under the scrutiny of his family and others who know him. It appears that with distance there would likely be not only new experiences, but fewer boundaries and restrictions and no one to lecture him about his new lifestyle.

- He "*wasted* his substance in *riotous* living." Oh, how much those two simple words convey about this young man. Here is another indicator of his immaturity and foolishness. Jesus didn't just say that he "spent" his inheritance. Rather he *wasted* it. Blew through it like there was no tomorrow, and likely reveled in every moment of it.

Jesus did not tell us how long it took for this foolish young man to blow through his inheritance, nor his response when he came to learn the true nature of his "friends." Jesus didn't say how long it took before this young man went from being "the man of the hour" to "the man with nothing."

Actually, his new state was much more than simply having nothing. Where he ended up when his fall was complete tells us that it was much worse than that. It is difficult for modern readers to fully understand the emotional revulsion that would come when a good Jewish boy from a solid and loving home ended up as a swineherd— a keeper of pigs. We need to remember that under the law of Moses, there were some foods that were forbidden to the Israelites. One of those was pork in any form.

By the time of Jesus, the restrictions on eating pork had turned into a deep cultural and religious abhorrence of anything even slightly connected to swine. Not only was eating any form of pork strictly forbidden, but by this time in history, even coming in contact with the animal, its food, or anything else the pigs had touched was strongly forbidden. Most Jewish villages at that time would not allow any pigs within them. So strong was this commitment that there are records of observant Jews suffering martyrdom rather than being forced to eat pork.

One historian gives us an example of this, speaking of the time when the Jews were oppressed by their foreign conquerors: "Jews were to perform the rituals of the Hellenistic [Greek] cults and were to eat the meat there, including the flesh of pigs. Those who refused were tortured before they were put to death" (Harry Thomas Frank, *Discovering the Biblical World*, 160).

Consider that as we contemplate our foolish young prodigal. He not only ended up accepting employment as a swine herd, because "no man gave to him," but he ended up living with the pigs and eating what the pigs ate! Anyone familiar with pigs knows they often step into the trough that holds their food, scattering it into the mud of the pigsty, which of course was more than just mud. They also root through the mud and offal to get at the food.

Considering the home that this young man had come from, his fall to this state is enough to make modern readers shudder.

THE PARABLE (CONT.)

And when he came to himself, he said, How many hired servants of my father's have bread enough and to spare, and I perish with hunger! I will arise and go to my father, and will say unto him, Father, I have sinned against heaven, and before thee, And am no more worthy to be called thy son: make me as one of thy hired servants. (Luke 15:17–19)

ANALYSIS AND APPLICATION (CONT.)

How profound and poignant is that simple phrase, "And when he came to himself." To say that he had been deeply humbled since leaving home would be an understatement. We can only imagine how many times he must have cursed himself and his stupidity for turning his back on what was a wonderful home and family. How many times had he thought of the bounteous meals back home, and the warm circle of family and friends who loved him? It is hard for us today to grasp how truly far this young man had fallen. But now he *came to himself.* What a terse way to describe the change he has undergone and how keenly he recognized just how foolish he had been.

In that shame and humiliation and deep regret, how often must he have thought about going home. But in this condition, in the sheer shame of his fall, he could not bring himself to face his family and chose to live with the pigs instead. But eventually he faced himself, acknowledged his pride and foolishness, and took personal responsibility for the choices that had led to his downfall.

That this was a true change of heart and not just coming from the misery of his situation is indicated by the fact that he had no expectation of being reinstated to his home and family. He had finally acknowledged to himself his own foolishness and recognized that his current state was the direct result of his own poor choices. The scriptural word for this kind of shame and remorse is "repentance." His self-acknowledgment that he was no longer worthy to be considered a family member is an indicator of the depths of his change of heart.

THE PARABLE (CONT.)

And he arose, and came to his father. But when he was yet a great way off, his father saw him, and had compassion, and ran, and fell on his neck, and kissed him. And the son said unto him, Father, I have sinned against heaven, and in thy sight, and am no more worthy to be called thy son. But the father said to his servants, Bring forth the best robe, and put it on him; and put a ring on his hand, and shoes on his feet: And bring hither the fatted calf, and kill it; and let us eat, and be merry: For this my son was dead, and is alive again; he was lost, and is found. And they began to be merry. (Luke 15:20–24)

ANALYSIS AND APPLICATION (CONT.)

Note how in that simple sentence, "when he was a great way off," the Savior describes the father. We receive a glimpse of the sorrow and pain the father has endured during his son's absence, and his love for his son. The insights Jesus gives us into the father's heart is one of the great lessons in scripture on how we approach those who stray.

It is interesting that Jesus doesn't say anything about the father going after his son to try and bring him back. Here are some things to consider about that:

- Some might assume that because the father felt angry and betrayed by his headstrong son, he had washed his hands of him, that he didn't care that much about the son.
- Or it could be that he accepted that his son had agency and was of age to make his own choices. There usually comes a point in the relationship between parents and children when the child needs to leave the family and strike out on his or her own.
- How was it that the father saw his son long before he reached home? Did he go out to the main road every day to watch? That seems unlikely. Did the father pay people on that highway to watch for his son and send him word? Or perhaps the prodigal son's Heavenly Father prompted his biological father to go out that day and watch? Jesus doesn't say, but that the father didn't wait until his foolish son had come all the way back before he ran to him says much about his love and patience and forgiveness.
- Jesus does not tell us what each element of the parable represents in our lives as He did in some of the parables. But surely, in this case, this father provides us with a type and symbol of our Heavenly Father, who patiently waits for those of His children who have chosen to make their own way in life and end up reaping the consequences of their own foolishness. And though they haven't come all the way back, He greets them with joy and tears while they are on their way— which is an important model for earthly parents as well.
- Another sweet model for those of us who are earthly parents and have had prodigals of our own is how the father greeted his son. It would have been so tempting to say things like, "See, my son. I told you that you were being a fool." Or, "Now do you believe that your mother and I know what we

are talking about?" Instead, the tears of sorrow that would have been shed on his departure are now tears of joy that he has returned.

- Is not this wise and loving father a type and shadow of our Heavenly Father and His perfect love for all His children?
- And isn't this also a type and shadow of those of us who come down to mortality? As Lehi taught, "Men are free according to the flesh. . . . And they are free to choose liberty and eternal life, . . . or to choose captivity and death" (2 Nephi 2:27). Or, to squander their inheritance in riotous living and eventually hit rock bottom. How grateful we should be for a Heavenly Father and His most beloved Son who are waiting for us to "come to ourselves" and come back home, where we will be greeted with joy and rejoicing.

But ironically, the story is not finished yet.

As already noted, this parable is one of the three parables Jesus taught about lost things. The prodigal son is different from the lost sheep, because he didn't just wander off while looking for green grass to eat; nor was he "dropped" through the carelessness or negligence of someone. He deliberately chose to find another life and break away from his family. His return to his family was a touching conclusion to his journey. It seems like a perfect end to the parable.

And yet it was not. Jesus continued and introduced us to another son in the family.

THE PARABLE (CONT.)

Now his elder son was in the field: and as he came and drew nigh to the house, he heard musick and dancing. And he called one of the servants, and asked what these things meant. And he said unto him, Thy brother is come; and thy father hath killed the fatted calf, because he hath received him safe and sound.

And he was angry, and would not go in: therefore came his father out, and entreated him. And he answering said to his father, Lo, these many years do I serve thee, neither transgressed I at any time thy commandment: and yet thou never gavest me a kid, that I might make merry with my friends: But as soon as this thy son was come, which hath devoured thy living with harlots, thou hast killed for him the fatted calf.

And he said unto him, Son, thou art ever with me, and all that I have is thine. It was meet that we should make merry, and be glad: for this thy brother was dead, and is alive again; and was lost, and is found. (Luke 15:25–32)

ANALYSIS AND APPLICATION (CONT.)

What an ironic and surprising turn in this touching family story. There is another son. One who never demanded that he get his inheritance early. One who stayed with his family and helped build up the estate. One who lost his younger brother and had no idea if he would ever see him again. And, surprisingly, one who reacted to the news of his brother's return with anger, bitterness, petulance, and resentment.

In this addendum to the parable, the father goes out to converse with another son, who is also lost in his own way, though he never left home. He was an older brother, so one would expect greater maturity and wisdom than the younger, more impetuous son. But instead we find a sour, resentful, pouty son who refuses to even come in and greet his brother or rejoice in his return. We have no reason to believe that he has been anything but faithful in the service to his father. And yet from what he says, it is almost like he envies the life that his brother had for a time.

This is a surprising turn in the story. Like the other two parables of lost things, in this parable the prodigal son is also found. He "came to himself" and returned to his family. A very happy ending. But immediately thereafter, Jesus adds the elder brother into the story. There is no indication that he has engaged in riotous living and all that implies. But he is lost in anger and irritation, lost from being able to rejoice in the return of his brother.

That seems puzzling in a way, for Jesus ends the parable with the father trying to persuade the petulant brother to come in, but He doesn't say whether he did or did not. He ends the story there.

What is Jesus trying to teach us with this addition to the story? We don't know all the answers, but here is one thing to keep in mind. Remember what triggered these three parables of the lost. The scribes and the Pharisees were complaining because Jesus was mingling with "sinners," i.e., those who were not as "faithful and righteous" as were the scribes and the Pharisees.

Though Jesus says no more about the elder brother, it must have been clear to the listeners there that day that this was a direct rebuke to the proud and haughty religious leaders who believed they were the only ones who pleased God and who resented those who refused to join them.

Though Luke doesn't record their reaction to what they heard, it seems safe to assume that they went away in a huff, untouched by the lesson taught and as rigid and unbending in their haughty pride as when they had come.

Elder Bruce R. McConkie, of the Quorum of the Twelve, said this of parables, which is especially true of the parable of the prodigal son:

> Parables are a call to investigate the truth; to learn more;
> to inquire into the spiritual realities, which, through them,
> are but dimly viewed. Parables start truth seekers out in the

direction of further light and knowledge and understanding; they invite men to ponder such truths as they are able to bear in the hope of learning more. Parables are a call to come unto Christ, to believe his doctrines, to live his laws, and to be saved in his kingdom. (*Mortal Messiah,* 2:245)

In that wise counsel, we can find many personal lessons and applications from the story of these two brothers. Because it is one of the best-known parables and because of the power of its message, leaders of the Church have often referred to it in their teaching, including this inspired message from Elder Neal A. Maxwell:

> Blessed, even so, are those of us who can trust God and be obedient without having to pass through each relevant learning experience. Yet each of us will end up with an impressive array of personal experiences as part of the luggage we take with us into the world to come. . . . Submission from experience is seen in the prodigal son's coming to a realization of his deplorable condition; he headed for home. Perchance did the prodigal, after wasting his inheritance, finally remember with humble appreciation his father's earlier generosity as the Holy Ghost preached to the prodigal from the pulpit of memory? (*Not My Will, But Thine,* 98)

NOTES

1. To long for; have a desire for, covet, seek after (see *Strong's Concordance,* 1909, 2372).

Chapter 12

Lazarus *and the* Rich Man

CONTEXT AND SETTING

As Jesus continued His mortal ministry, Luke recorded another parable that provides us with a powerful model of how we are to minister and to whom we should minister. Luke recorded it immediately following the parable of the prodigal son with no information on the setting or what may have prompted Jesus to share this parable, which the chapter introduction for Luke 16 called "the parable of the unjust steward." Luke introduced it with this short explanation: "And he said also unto his disciples. . . ." then immediately launched into this parable.

The phrase "said *also*" suggests that this might have immediately followed the parable of the prodigal son and his petulant brother. That supposition is supported by the fact that when Jesus gave the intended lesson of the parable, there were Pharisees present who began to "deride" Jesus, according to Luke. That too seems to suggest this is the same day, but not conclusively.

But in the parable itself, there is nothing that seems to clearly link it to the story of the prodigal son and his surly brother. We shall study the parable of the unjust steward in the next section, which is a study of parables that focus on preparing ourselves for the Second Coming of Christ.

The parable begins with the account of a steward who was in charge of a successful man's business and was caught cheating his master by falsifying the entries in the book containing the business records. When his master discovered what the steward was doing, he demanded an accounting of him. Jesus used what the steward did to prepare for the termination of his employment as a lesson in setting priorities and preparing for the future.

The Pharisees who were there that day bristled at the implication that they were like the unjust steward in that they too were covetous. Jesus then gave examples of where they were not in harmony with the will of God (see Luke 16:13–18).

As this point, Jesus was well along in His three-year ministry and He had drawn thousands to Him and to His teachings. He often publicly criticized the leaders of the two most popular sects at that time, the Sadducees and the Pharisees. He accused them of turning the law of Moses into a codified set of restrictive laws that were so burdensome that most of the common people turned away from these two sects. Some of these religious leaders used their expertise in the law and their influence to extort money, seize property—including that of widows—and make themselves the rich and powerful elite of the Jews. Among the common people there was much bitter resentment of this gross hypocrisy, and often they were delighted when Jesus openly condemned the Sadducees and the Pharisees. And the more the people turned to Jesus and turned away from them, the more Jesus became a direct threat to their power, influence, and wealthy lifestyle.

This is the context that brought forth the parable of Lazarus and the rich man.

THE PARABLE

There was a certain rich man, which was clothed in purple and fine linen, and fared sumptuously every day: And there was a certain beggar named Lazarus, which was laid at his gate, full of sores, and desiring to be fed with the crumbs which fell from the rich man's table: moreover the dogs came and licked his sores. And it came to pass, that the beggar died, and was carried by the angels into Abraham's bosom: the rich man also died, and was buried;

And in hell he lift up his eyes, being in torments, and seeth Abraham afar off, and Lazarus in his bosom. And he cried and said, Father Abraham, have mercy on me, and send Lazarus, that he may dip the tip of his finger in water, and cool my tongue; for I am tormented in this flame.

But Abraham said, Son, remember that thou in thy lifetime receivedst thy good things, and likewise Lazarus evil things: but now he is comforted, and thou art tormented. And beside all this, between us and you there is a great gulf fixed: so that they which would pass from hence to you cannot; neither can they pass to us, that would come from thence.

Then he said, I pray thee therefore, father, that thou wouldest send him to my father's house:

For I have five brethren; that he may testify unto them, lest they also come into this place of torment. Abraham saith unto him, They have Moses and the prophets; let them hear them.

And he said, Nay, father Abraham: but if one went unto them from the dead, they will repent.

And he said unto him, If they hear not Moses and the prophets, neither will they be persuaded, though one rose from the dead. (Luke 16:19–31)

ANALYSIS

There are several points of sweet and bitter irony in the description Jesus gave of these two men:

- The wealthy and influential man is given no name, while the most wretched of beggars is named Lazarus, which in Hebrew means "God helps." From time immemorial, two words often used to describe the super wealthy are *rich* and *famous*. In our day, the names of these über-wealthy men and women are known worldwide. Yet this rich and powerful man was not named at all.

- The rich man was clothed in purple and linen, the two most expensive fabrics of the ancient world. Often they were owned only by royalty. Though it doesn't say this, Lazarus was most likely in filthy rags.

- The rich man "fared sumptuously." Every day was a banquet for the rich man. Lazarus got his meager nourishment from the crumbs left over from the banquets of the rich man.

- No mention was made of any health problems the rich man had, whereas Lazarus was piteously described as being "full of sores" and so weak that he couldn't fight off the dogs from licking at those sores.

- The gruesome description of the wretchedness of Lazarus's situation starkly showed the disparity between the two men, which was now reversed. Lazarus was taken up to Abraham's bosom by angels. In Bible times the bosom was often used symbolically as a place of comfort and safety. One reason for this is that babies had been fed and nourished at the breasts of their mothers for generations. Also, in the clothing of those days, a man's tunic was not fastened with buttons but was held shut by a belt at his waist. This left his chest covered but only by overlapping cloth, not buttons or fasteners. Shepherds would often take newborn lambs into their bosom to keep them warm on cold nights. When people embrace in friendship or love, their bosoms touch. Thus, the bosom is a symbol of intimacy, safety, comfort, nurturing, and love. Jesus is described as being in the "bosom of the Father" (D&C 76:13).

- Abraham was seen as one of the greatest of the Old Testament prophets. One of his titles was "father of the faithful" (D&C 138:41). Therefore, to be in "Abraham's bosom" signified being in a place of love, safety, and warmth reserved only for the most faithful—in a word, to be in what we now call paradise.

- For the rich, who would be buried with great spectacle in fabulous tombs, the description of the rich man's fate, summed up in five stark words—"he died and was buried"—would have come as a terrible insult to their pride and expectations.

In summary, the sharp contrast drawn by Jesus between these two men in life was dramatic. And so it was proved to be at their death, only completely reversed. How bitter that must have been for the Pharisees listening to Jesus that day, for they knew full well that Jesus was describing their own pride and arrogance.

APPLICATION

One of the traits commonly found among some of the wealthy and powerful is what is known as a sense of entitlement or privilege. They are so used to being waited on hand and foot every day of their lives and having their every whim gratified that some come to actually believe they are inherently superior to others, which gives them some kind of divine rights. And often they see their enormous wealth as proof of that favored status.

We see this same subconscious attitude in the rich man here.

Once he sees where he is, in his shock and bewilderment, he calls out to Abraham for his help. How ironic. Even here, he assumes that Abraham, one of the greatest prophets who ever lived, can be ordered about like a private servant. Even more insightful is that he doesn't even say please!

Think about that for a minute. In those years when Lazarus lay helpless at his front door, the rich man never gave him a second thought. He never did anything for him. He never offered him food, never invited him to come in out of the rain, and very likely never even knew his name. And now, even after he has died, we see that same natural arrogance and privileged expectation that everyone around him is standing there just waiting to fill his every need.

He seems not to even be amazed that Lazarus is no longer an invalid but demands that he come and take care of him and his needs.

How enlightening this is to the character of the rich man. He has passed from life into the spirit world and his situation is drastically changed. Yet his arrogance and insensitivity haven't changed at all.

Abraham's response was short and to the point. First, he made it clear to the rich man that his change in status was a direct result of his life on earth (see Luke 16:25). Second, he confirmed that joy comes from keeping the commandments and living one's life in harmony with God's will, not from riches and influence (see v. 25). Evidently, that hadn't yet registered in the rich man's mind.

In our theology, we believe that after death we can continue to change and repent and make things right again. But the rich man was not thinking of any of that yet. At this point, his whole focus was on his discomfort, and he demanded that someone get him a glass of water.

If the parable had ended there, it would have been an enriching teaching experience for those listening to Jesus on that day. But Jesus had one more lesson to teach His disciples and the haughty and proud Pharisees. It is a lesson for us today as well.

Finally, the reality of the unnamed rich man's circumstances began to settle into his consciousness and he began to understand the enormity of his failures back on earth. It is commendable that he thought of his family. But again, we see his inherent arrogance. He now pleads with Abraham to send someone down to warn his brothers who, evidently, are very much like him. But Abraham reminded him that his brothers had the scriptures and the teachings of the prophets. They didn't need a tutor from the spirit world. They could learn from the sacred writ.

But the rich man, who clearly knew the nature of his brothers because they were very much like he was, finally seems to understand what his choices in life mean for him now in the spirit world. And yet—and this is another irony in his thinking—he knows his brothers are not going to be any more responsive to what the scriptures have to say than he did. But if Abraham were to send Lazarus down to the family, that might be shock enough to give them a wake-up call. Alas, Abraham wisely notes that this is not how human nature works.

As we close our study of this remarkable parable, we note that this was not meant to be an automatic condemnation of people who have been blessed with great wealth. There are numerous individuals in the scriptures who had great wealth—Abraham being one of them—who were paragons of faith and service.

The point Jesus was making in this parable comes back to the concept of ministering to others in need. Those in need are all around us. And the greater our resources, the greater is our opportunity to do good. If we ignore that obligation it will have sobering consequences on our spiritual development when it is our time to pass through the veil and start a new phase of living.

Elder James E. Talmage, in his seminal work *Jesus the Christ*, noted this about the parable:

> The rich man's fate was not the effect of riches, nor was the rest into which Lazarus entered the resultant of poverty. Failure to use his wealth aright, and selfish satisfaction with the sensuous enjoyment of earthly things to the exclusion of all concern for the needs or privations of his fellows, brought the one under condemnation; while patience in suffering, faith in God and such righteous life as is implied though not expressed, insured happiness to the other. The proud self-sufficiency of the rich man, who lacked nothing that wealth could furnish and who kept aloof from the needy and suffering, was his besetting sin. The aloofness of the Pharisees, on which indeed they prided themselves, as their very name, signifying "separatists," expressed, was thus condemned. The parable teaches the continuation of individual existence after death, and the relation of cause to effect between the life one leads in mortality and the state awaiting him beyond. (*Jesus the Christ*, 468–469)

This message from Jesus in the parable of Lazarus and the rich man is unmistakably clear. If we have the means and ignore those in need, there will be sobering consequences on our spiritual growth after we die. It is a message that is confirmed over and over in the scriptures. In gratitude for the blessings we receive from His bounteous hand, we all are asked again and again to reach out and bless the lives of others:

- Look to and administer to the relief of the poor and the needy (see D&C 38:35).
- Remember and consecrate our properties to the poor (see D&C 42:30).

- Visit and administer to the relief of the poor and the needy (see D&C 44:6).

- Remember in all things the poor, the needy, the sick, and the afflicted (see D&C 52:40).

- Provide for the widows, the orphans, and the poor (see D&C 83:6).

- Search after and administer to the wants [not just the needs] of the poor (see D&C 84:112).

- Impart of our substance to the poor and the afflicted (see D&C 105:3).

- Remember your imperative duty to the widows and the fatherless (see D&C 123:9).

- Administer blessings on the heads of poor (see D&C 124:21).

- Plead the cause of the poor and the needy (see D&C 124:75).

- Support the cause of the poor (see D&C 124:89).

- Bear an equal proportion of care for the poor, the widows, the fatherless, and the soldiers' [of the Mormon Battalion] families (D&C 136:8).

- "Wherefore, be faithful; stand in the office which I have appointed unto you; succor the weak, lift up the hands which hang down, and strengthen the feeble knees" (D&C 81:5; see also Job 4:4; Isaiah, 35:3; Hebrews 12:12).

- "And now, . . . for the sake of retaining a remission of your sins from day to day, that ye may walk guiltless before God . . . impart of your substance to the poor, every man according to that which he hath, such as feeding the hungry, clothing the naked, visiting the sick and administering to their relief, both spiritually and temporally, according to their wants"[1] (Mosiah 4:26).

As noted in an earlier chapter, Jesus defined His own mission in terms of ministering to those in need (see Luke 4:16–20). And throughout His mortal ministry, He admonished His disciples to follow His example, which He exhibited constantly throughout the three years of His mortal ministry.

We also noted that in 2018, after being sustained as President of the Church, President Russell M. Nelson began a new emphasis on how we minister to others within the Church. This teaching strongly supports what we are taught in the parable of Lazarus and the rich man. President Nelson said: "A hallmark of the Lord's true and living Church will always be an organized, directed effort to minister to individual children of God and their families. Because it is His Church, we as His servants will minister to the one, just as He did. We will minister in His name, with His power and authority, and with His loving-kindness ("Ministering with the Power and Authority of God," *Ensign*, May 2018).

In the priesthood session of that same conference, President Henry B. Eyring said:

> It seems to me that we receive the Holy Spirit best when we are focused on serving others. That is why we have the priesthood responsibility to serve for the Savior. When we are engaged in service to others, we think less about ourselves, and the Holy Ghost can more readily come to us and help us in our lifelong quest to have the gift of charity bestowed upon us. I bear you my witness that the Lord has already begun a great step forward in His plan for us to become even more inspired and charitable in our priesthood ministering service. ("Inspired Ministering," *Ensign*, May 2018)

At the time the change from home teaching to ministering was introduced, I was serving on the high council of our stake. In the months that followed, the stake presidency asked us to speak on ministering when we were assigned to speak in various ward sacrament meetings. We were curious about how the Church members were responding to President Nelson's call for us to minister in a higher and holier way. Sadly, there were some examples of members not rising to the challenge to administer to others. Here are some of the reports shared with me.

One woman in a ward had not been active for years, but loved having her visiting teachers come to visit her each month. "It helps me keep in touch with the Lord," she would often say. When the ministering program began, her ministering sisters were changed, much to her disappointment. Eight months later she had not had any contact from either of her new ministering sisters.

A widow in another ward arose one morning to find that her toilet was plugged. She called two brethren who had told her they had been assigned as her ministering brothers and asked if they could help. Both were very apologetic but said that they were too busy to do that right then. Discouraged, she called her former bishop, who had been her home teacher for several years. Half an hour later, the problem was solved.

I am happy to say that there were some wonderful reports too. Another widow reported that every morning after a snowstorm, she would wake up to find her sidewalks and driveways cleaned of the snow. She wondered who it was and asked several women in neighborhood if it was their husbands or sons doing it. All said that it was not.

Finally, after one snowstorm, she got up early and watched through the curtains out the window. Soon she saw a twelve-year-old boy who lived a few houses down from her come with his shovel and go to work. When she called his mother later that day to thank her, the mother was astonished. She'd had no idea that her son was doing that.

Here is an especially sweet account that shows that many of the youth are responding to President Nelson's call to ministering service. A married granddaughter shared this story that occurred in her ward.

She told of a single mother who had four young and energetic children. My granddaughter said that each Sunday at sacrament meeting they would see this mother come in with her children and find a bench. Soon the children were wiggling and talking to each other, occasionally punching a brother or sister on the arm. Others in the ward watched this with sympathy, admiring her for her faithfulness in not giving up.

But one morning, my granddaughter watched as a short time after the family was seated, another family came into the chapel. They had two teenage daughters. As they entered the chapel the parents found a seat, but the girls leaned down and whispered something to them, then went to the young mother and with a smile said, "Would you like us to sit with your family and help with the children?"

One can only imagine what that meant to the mother as that became the pattern every Sabbath thereafter. Later, my granddaughter spoke to the girls' mother and asked her if this had been a suggestion from their parents. "No," came the reply. "We were surprised when they did that. When I asked my girls what prompted them to do that, their answer was, 'President Nelson encouraged us to find ways to minister to those in need. So we did.'"

The reminder to minister to those in need is truly one of the sweet aspects of the many parables Jesus has given us.

In closing this section, let us note the counsel given in a general conference by Sister Sharon Eubank, First Counselor in the Relief

Society General Presidency. Sister Eubank is also in charge of the Humanitarian Services of The Church of Jesus Christ of Latter-day Saints. She helps coordinate providing services to people all around the world, including both members of the Church and those who are not members. She gave this powerful reminder of how important this work is to the Savior:

> The Church of Jesus Christ is under divine mandate to care for the poor. It is one of the pillars of the work of salvation and exaltation. What was true during the days of Alma is certainly true for us: "And thus, in their prosperous circumstances, they did not send away any who were naked, or that were hungry, or that were athirst, or that were sick, or that had not been nourished; and they did not set their hearts upon riches; therefore they were liberal to all, both old and young, both bond and free, both male and female, whether out of the church or in the church, having no respect to persons as to those who stood in need (Alma 1:30). ("I Pray He'll Use Us," *Liahona*, November 2021)

In closing we again remember that day in Nazareth when Jesus went to the pulpit and read these words from Isaiah:

> The Spirit of the Lord is upon me, because he hath anointed me to preach the gospel to the poor; he hath sent me to heal the brokenhearted, to preach deliverance to the captives, and recovering of sight to the blind, to set at liberty them that are bruised, To preach the acceptable year of the Lord. (Luke 4:18–19)

He then closed the book, looked out on those present, and declared, "This day is this scripture fulfilled in your ears" (Luke 4:21). In our day, when ministering is a major focus of the Church, may we each seek to more diligently follow the example of the Master, which Peter described in five simple words: "[He] went about doing good" (Acts 10:38).

NOTES

1. "Wants" seems to be used here not to suggest that the poor be given whatever they desire, but in the sense of, "they are in need."

Part IV

Preparation *for*
Christ's Coming

Chapter 13

The Wheat *and the* Tares

CONTEXT AND SETTING

The context and setting for this parable are the same as the context and setting for the parable of the soils (see chapter 4). When Jesus finished that parable of the soils, His disciples asked Him to help them understand why He taught the people in parables. In brief, Jesus explained that one of the reasons He used parables was that people had different levels of readiness. For those seeking spiritual truth and enlightenment, they could be powerful teaching moments. Those who weren't interested in such things would think that they were just a nice story. In other words, one of the virtues of parables is that they can *reveal* spiritual truth to some while they *conceal* those principles to those who are not ready for them.

After He taught them that principle, Jesus went through the parable of the soils and explained what each item in the story represented. Jesus seems to have made them understand, for He went on to give them seven more parables at that same time, one of which was the parable we shall study in this chapter, the parable of the wheat and the tares.

Matthew noted that this method of teaching had been prophesied centuries before in relationship to the coming Messiah when the

Psalmist said: "I will open my mouth in a parable: I will utter dark sayings of old: which we have heard and known, and our fathers have told us" (Psalm 78:2–3).

However, in the case of the parable of the wheat and the tares, while the same principles apply to it as well, it is, in one way, unique from all of the other parables Jesus taught while on earth.

In our dispensation, through the Prophet Joseph Smith, the Lord blessed us with new holy scripture and had the Prophet make many changes in the Bible to clarify some passages and correct others. We know that effort now as the Joseph Smith Translation of the Bible (JST). On December 6, 1832, the Lord gave Joseph an updated version of one of the parables He had taught during His mortal ministry. Other parables were often mentioned, and a few were even quoted in modern scripture, but only one parable was rewritten to update it for our day. That parable was the parable of the wheat and the tares.

To better understand the significance of that unique nature of this particular parable, we shall carefully examine both the New Testament version and the Doctrine and Covenant version.

THE PARABLE (KING JAMES VERSION– WITH JST CHANGES INCLUDED)[1]

Another parable put he forth unto them, saying, The kingdom of heaven is likened unto a man which sowed good seed in his field: But while men slept, his enemy came and sowed tares among the wheat, and went his way.

But when the blade was sprung up, and brought forth fruit, then appeared the tares also. So the servants of the householder came and said unto him, Sir, didst not thou sow good seed in thy field? from whence then hath it tares?

He said unto them, An enemy hath done this. The servants

said unto him, Wilt thou then that we go and gather them up? But he said, Nay; lest while ye gather up the tares, ye root up also the wheat with them. Let both grow together until the harvest: and in the time of harvest I will say to the reapers, **Gather ye together first the wheat into my barn: and the tares are bound in bundles to be burned,** and bind them in bundles to burn them: but gather the wheat into my barn (Matthew 13:24–30; JST Matthew 13:29).

ANALYSIS

The first question we need to answer if we are to understand the parable is, "What are tares?" One Bible scholar gave this detailed definition:

> The tares in the verse are *zizanion* in Greek. This word denotes the weed commonly known as "darnel," or "bearded darnel." Its official name is *Lolium temulentum.* The darnel before it comes into ear *is very similar in appearance to wheat.* . . . These stalks if sown designedly throughout the fields would be inseparable from the wheat . . . [for] they are at first sight hardly distinguishable. . . . *The closest scrutiny will often fail to detect them.* . . . The grains of the *Lolium temulentum,* if eaten, produce convulsions, and even death (Smith's Bible Dictionary, 674).

Another scholar added this insight: "The seeds, though often poisonous to humans on account of parasitic growths in them, are sold as chicken's food. When harvest approaches and the tares can be distinguished, they are carefully weeded out by hand" (James Hastings, *Dictionary of the Bible,* 893).

In response to His disciples' query about what the parable of the soils meant, Jesus went through the key elements one by one.

Thankfully, He did the same thing with this parable, offering some of the possible interpretations for these scriptures (see Matthew 13:37–43). Here is His explanation, put into the side-by-side format.

The sower of the good seed	The Son of Man, a title for Jesus Christ. Since Jesus once said that He and His Father were one, both are part of this. And since They extend Their power and authority to faithful followers, we could say that their servants are also included here. Obviously, those called to serve in this work, such as the Twelve Apostles and other members of the kingdom, also partake of this work.
The field	The world in which we live, and thus all mankind.
The good seed	In the parable of the sower, the seed represented the gospel, so all of that seed was "good." Here Jesus taught that it represents the children of the kingdom, i.e., those who are part of the Lord's covenant people.
The tares	The children (or followers) of the wicked one, i.e., Satan.
Sower of the tares	Satan, and those who embrace his work.
The harvest	The end of the world; or, from the JST, the destruction of the wicked. "World" could refer to worldliness and not just the earth itself. The JST addition here is significant.

The reapers	The angels, or, from the JST, the messengers sent down from heaven. These are servants of the most High God. This could include angels from any dispensation of the gospel, ancient or modern, as well as people now living on earth. The Lord gives us no further information on who these angels are.
Tares gathered and burned	Matthew's version states that the tares—the wicked—are gathered and burned in the fire at the end of the world, but the JST changes that to "or the destruction of the wicked." The JST also gives us a time marker for this event: "For in that day, before the Son of man shall come. . . ." So while the parable was applicable in other ages, it is especially so in our time.
Gather out of his kingdom	The KJV says all things that offend and do iniquity shall be cast out. The JST adds two insights here. They shall be cast out among the wicked; and there shall be wailing and gnashing of teeth, for the world shall be burned with fire.
Wheat gathered into barns	The faithful (probably of all times and dispensations), including those who greatly multiplied the work in the early history of Christianity. All will be separated and blessed with a multiplicity of blessings.
Tares burned in the fire	This takes place at the end of the world, or, according to the JST, is the destruction of the

wicked. The Son of Man gathers up all that "offend and do iniquity" and casts them into a literal destruction by fire. "They who are filthy are the devil and his angels; and they shall go away into everlasting fire, prepared for them; and *their torment is as* a lake of fire and brimstone, whose flame ascendeth up forever and ever and has no end. . . . [The] lake of fire and brimstone . . . is *endless torment*" (2 Nephi 9:16, 19; emphasis added). Remember also that "endless torment" is not a punishment that lasts for all of eternity but rather is called that because one of God's titles is Endless (see D&C 19:10–12). The endless torment is God's torment, not necessarily flames that go on forever.

ANALYSIS

Not long after The Church of Jesus Christ of Latter-day Saints was organized in 1830, the Lord told Joseph Smith to work on the King James Version of the Bible, correcting by inspiration some things that had been lost or altered down through time. As mentioned previously, we now call his inspired reworking of the Bible the Joseph Smith Translation (JST).

In the parable of the sower discussed earlier, Joseph Smith made only a few minor changes to the biblical text. However, in the parable of the wheat and the tares, there are several significant changes in the JST, as we have seen. These add significantly to our understanding of the parable and show that the parable is still relevant to our day.

But the Lord did more than inspire Joseph to correct the ancient text. Through revelation, He gave Joseph a *new* version of the parable, which has been updated to our day and time (see D&C 86). Though other parables are mentioned or cited in the Doctrine and Covenants, this is the only parable from the time of Jesus that was significantly revised for our day. Therefore, this parable is unique and has great value for our generation.

THE PARABLE (DOCTRINE AND COVENANTS VERSION)

Verily, thus saith the Lord unto you my servants, concerning the parable of the wheat and of the tares: Behold, verily I say, the field was the world, and the apostles were the sowers of the seed; And after they have fallen asleep the great persecutor of the church, the apostate, the whore, even Babylon, that maketh all nations to drink of her cup, in whose hearts the enemy, even Satan, sitteth to reign—behold he soweth the tares; wherefore, the tares choke the wheat and drive the church into the wilderness.

But behold, in the last days, even now while the Lord is beginning to bring forth the word, and the blade is springing up and is yet tender—Behold, verily I say unto you, the angels are crying unto the Lord day and night, who are ready and waiting to be sent forth to reap down the fields; But the Lord saith unto them, pluck not up the tares while the blade is yet tender (for verily your faith is weak), lest you destroy the wheat also.

Therefore, let the wheat and the tares grow together until the harvest is fully ripe; then ye shall first gather out the wheat from among the tares, and after the gathering of the wheat, behold and lo, the tares are bound in bundles, and the field remaineth to be burned. Therefore, thus saith the Lord unto you, with whom the priesthood hath continued through the lineage of your fathers—

For ye are lawful heirs, according to the flesh, and have been hid from the world with Christ in God—Therefore your life and the priesthood have remained, and must needs remain through you and your lineage until the restoration of all things spoken by the mouths of all the holy prophets since the world began. Therefore, blessed are ye if ye continue in my goodness, a light unto the Gentiles, and through this priesthood, a savior unto my people Israel. The Lord hath said it. Amen. (D&C 86:1–11)

ANALYSIS

When we read the prophecies found in the scriptures, a natural question often comes to mind: "Do we know when that prophecy will come to pass?" In the vast majority of cases, the answer is no, at least not with any specificity. But this prophecy is unique, and we do have such a marker.

When Jesus first gave this parable back in His day, in His explanation of each element of the parable He explained that the reaping of the tares represented that time when "the Son of man shall send forth his angels, and they shall gather out of his kingdom *all things that offend* and *them which do iniquity*" (Matthew 13:41; emphasis added).

When we consider how many things there are in this world that offend the perfections of God, and how many times in history the world has chosen iniquity over obedience to the laws of the gospel, this promise is sobering indeed.

So a key consideration for us living in the latter days is this: This updated parable foretells a time when the angels of judgment will be loosed to carry out their mission of reaping down the fields, or bringing God's judgment down upon the world. Do we have any idea of when that time will come?

Surprisingly, the answer is yes. And that answer may be more specific than most people might expect. This is so because in our dispensation, the Savior's "revised update" of the parable of the wheat and the tares came in the form of a revelation given to the Prophet Joseph Smith that is now found in the Doctrine and Covenants, section 86. Joseph was given not only an updated parable but also the description of what those key elements represented.

Then, even more astonishing, about sixty years after that revelation, President Wilford Woodruff, the prophet and President of The Church of Jesus Christ of Latter-day Saints at that time, was given addition information on the parable, including a specific marker on when those times of judgment would begin.

The first seven verses of section 86 contain an updated explanation of the key elements of the parable. The last four verses are an admonition given through Joseph Smith to the members of the Church, which clearly were not just for the members at the time it was given but for future generations as well. Readers are encouraged to carefully compare the revelation in the Doctrine and Covenants to the original version in Matthew, as well as the JST alterations to that version. There is much to be learned in such a study.

APPLICATION

An observation before we examine the further things the Lord has revealed about this parable. Any serious student of scripture should understand that the word of the Lord is filled with numerous voices. There is a voice of hope and a voice of despair; a voice of joy and a voice of sorrow; a voice of love and compassion and a voice of anger and condemnation.

Two voices that are especially prevalent throughout the four standard works are what we might think of as a *voice of promise* and a *voice of warning*. There are numerous examples of this, and the parable of the wheat and the tares is a good one. For example:

Warning: "The Son of man shall send forth his angels, and they shall gather out of his kingdom all things that offend, and them which do iniquity; and shall cast them into a furnace of fire" (Matthew 13:41–42).

Promise: "Then shall the righteous shine forth as the sun in the kingdom of their Father" (Matthew 13:43).

In the modern version of the parable we find a similar structure:

Warning: "Behold, verily I say unto you, the angels are crying unto the Lord day and night, who are ready and waiting to be sent forth to reap down the fields" (D&C 86:5).

Promise: "Blessed are ye if ye continue in my goodness, a light unto the Gentiles, and through this priesthood, a savior unto my people Israel" (D&C 86:11).

Often these promises and warnings also describe times of separation or times of inclusion for the Father's children. President Joseph Fielding Smith defined this separation and what decides where we go when we are separated.

The time will come, just as sure as we live, that *there will be a separation between the righteous and the unrighteous*. Those who will not keep the law of the Lord will deny the faith, for *he will withdraw his Spirit from them* if they do not repent, after laboring with them and doing all that is possible to keep them in the line of duty. *He will withdraw his Spirit from them and they will be left unto themselves.* They must take one side or the other, for this separation must surely come. (*Doctrines of Salvation*, 3:15; emphasis added)

The promises are as joyous as the warnings are grim. Note this promise in the Doctrine and Covenants: "Learn that he who doeth the works of righteousness shall receive his reward, *even peace in this world, and eternal life in the world to come*" (D&C 59:23; emphasis added).

Or consider this promise in the parable of the soils, which was given at the same time as the parable of the wheat and the tares. After describing how the wicked will be cast into a furnace of fire, the Lord then says of the righteous: "Then shall the righteous shine forth as the sun in the kingdom of their Father" (Matthew 13:42–43).

And there it is. *Separation* and *exclusion* as opposed to *preparation* and *inclusion*. That is clearly a message in the parable of the wheat and tares. "And they [the angels of judgment] shall **gather out of his kingdom all things that offend**, and them which do iniquity, and shall cast them **out among the wicked**" (JST, Matthew 13:41–42).

But there is an important question raised by this modern update of the parable. It is this: Now that we know that the angels who are called to reap down the fields were primarily to come in our day and time, not just back two thousand years ago, do we have any more specific information on when those angels of judgment will be loosed—or if they *have been loosed*? Or, to put it another way, since it has been almost two hundred years since this update to the parable of the wheat and tares was given, is it possible that the time for this reaping of the fields has come?

The answer to both questions is yes!

In a revelation given to the Saints on January 2, 1831, the Lord made another reference to the parable of the wheat and the tares:

All flesh is corrupted before me; and the powers of darkness prevail upon the earth, among the children of men, in the presence of all the hosts of heaven—Which causeth silence to reign, and all eternity is pained, and *the angels are waiting the great command to reap down the earth*, to gather the tares that they may be burned. (D&C 38:11–12; emphasis added)

So, in 1831, the angels were still awaiting the call to begin their work. And as we have seen in Doctrine and Covenants 86, the angels were still awaiting their call in late 1832. Here, however, the Lord suggests that the time of holding back the angels of judgment was soon to end. Joseph Smith said about that time:

We learn by this parable, not only the setting up of the Kingdom in the days of the Savior, which is represented by the good seed, which produced fruit, but also the corruptions of the Church, which are represented by the tares, which were sown by the enemy, which His disciples would fain have plucked up, or cleansed the Church of, if their views had been favored by the Savior. But He, knowing all things, says, Not so. As much as to say, your views are not correct, the Church is in its infancy, and if you take this rash step, you will destroy the wheat, or the Church, with the tares; therefore it is better to let them grow together until the harvest, or the end of the world, which means the destruction of the wicked, which is not yet fulfilled. (*Teachings*, 97)

Then, after more than half a century had come and gone, something quite electrifying took place. Wilford Woodruff, who had been called to the holy Apostleship by Joseph Smith, was now serving as the fourth President of The Church of Jesus Christ of Latter-day Saints. On April 6, 1893, exactly forty years after the cornerstone had been laid for the Salt Lake Temple, the sacred building was formally dedicated, led by President Woodruff. Since this was long before the days of radio and television and satellite transmissions, it was decided that there would be forty-one dedicatory sessions to accommodate those who were invited to attend.

Somewhere during those services, perhaps in a meeting with the First Presidency and the Twelve, President Woodruff made a startling declaration. This was reported by President Joseph Fielding Smith when he was a member of the Quorum of the Twelve Apostles:

> One theme that was on the mind of President Wilford Woodruff more than any other for a number of years before his death—in fact, from the time of the dedication of the [Salt Lake] Temple until his death—was this theme of the parable of the wheat and tares. . . . The first he said it, was at the time of the dedication of the Temple in 1893. (*Signs of the Times*, 112, 114)[2]

Though President Smith did not share many details of what President Woodruff said at the temple dedication that would indicate why he referenced the parable of the wheat and the tares, fortunately, President Woodruff spoke of it several times afterward, confirming what Joseph Fielding Smith had reported. One of those times was in 1894, when President Woodruff spoke to a group of temple workers in Salt Lake City. The language he used clearly shows that he was referring to the parable of the wheat and the tares:

> I want to bear testimony to you that God has held the angels of destruction for many years, lest they should reap down the wheat with the tares. But I want to tell you now, that those angels have left the portals of heaven, and they stand over this people and this nation now, and are hovering over the earth waiting to pour out the judgments. And

from this very day they shall be poured out. Calamities and troubles are increasing in the earth. . . . If you do your duty, and I do my duty, we'll have protection, and shall pass through the afflictions in peace and safety. (Wilford Woodruff, "The Temple Workers' Excursion," June 24, 1894, reported by Susan Young Gates, *The Young Woman's Journal*, Vol. 5, pp. 512–513. Also in *Discourses*, 229–30)

Three months later, in fall general conference, President Woodruff again spoke of the angels who had been held back by the Lord and explained what was happening. He began by speaking of what appeared to be judgments coming upon the world:

What is the matter with the world today? What has created this change that we see coming over the world? Why these terrible earthquakes, tornadoes, and judgments? What is the meaning of all these mighty events that are taking place? The meaning is, these angels that have been held for many years in the temple of our God have got their liberty to go out and commence their mission and their work in the earth, and they are here today in the earth. (Wilford Woodruff, *Millennial Star*, Vol. 56, p. 643, October 8, 1894)

Two years after that, once again in general conference, President Woodruff returned to this subject and was even more specific than before about the judgments:

I want to bear testimony to this congregation, and to the heavens and the earth, that the day is come when those angels are privileged to go forth and commence their work. They are laboring in the United States of America; they are laboring among the nations of the earth; and they will continue. We need not marvel or wonder at anything that is transpiring

in the earth. . . . In our day these things will come to pass. I
heard the Prophet Joseph bear his testimony to these events
that would transpire in the earth. . . . We cannot draw a veil
over the events that await this generation. No man that is
inspired by the Spirit and power of God can close his ears, his
eyes or his lips to these things. (Wilford Woodruff, *Millennial
Star*, Vol. 58, p. 739, November 19, 1896)

One of the surprising things about what President Woodruff
said about these angels was that they were unleashing "calamities
and troubles," "terrible earthquakes," "tornadoes," and "judgments,"
suggesting the idea that one way the judgments of God will be
brought to pass will be through natural disasters and calamities, as
prophesied so often in the scriptures.

In this dispensation, the Lord has said that He would speak to
the nations of the earth "by the mouth of my servants, and *by the
ministering of angels*, and my mine own voice, and by the voice of
thunderings, and by the voice of lightnings, and by the voice of tem-
pests, and by the voice of earthquakes, and great hailstorms, and by
the voice of famines and pestilences of every kind. . . . Behold, the
day has come, when the cup of the wrath of mine indignation is
full" (D&C 43:25–26; emphasis added).

Obviously, the connection between "the judgments of God,"
and what we call "natural disasters" is a strong one. Based on what
President Woodruff taught about the parable of the wheat and the
tares, one thing that the angels were going to unleash upon the earth
were various kinds of natural disasters and other forms of tribulation. And from the date of the revelation given to Joseph Smith,
now Doctrine and Covenants 86 (December 6, 1832) to the time
President Woodruff received the revelation that the angels of judgment had been released (April 1890), we can say with considerable
assurance that the angels of judgment in the parable were released to

start the judgments in our dispensation. There may have been some fulfillment during the Christ's day, but it is certainly being fulfilled in our dispensation.

This should not come as surprise, for the scriptures frequently describe various kinds of natural disasters that have happened in the past and often describe such phenomena in our day. And while that promise is one that we view with some trepidation, we should view the parable as a blessing, for it is one of the signs of the times that Jesus Himself gave to His people. Notice His direction that we should do so—i.e., we should watch for those signs—with faith and a hope. In another revelation to Joseph Smith, Jesus recounted that when He was giving the Twelve the Olivet Discourse, which foretold of many terrible things to come, He encouraged them that they should "be not troubled" (D&C 45:35).

Even today, we find ourselves wondering, "How can we not be troubled when we hear of such grim things as He was predicting for their day and for ours?" Jesus gave the answer a few verses later: "And it shall come to pass that he that feareth me shall be looking forth for the great day of the Lord to come, even for the signs of the coming of the Son of Man" (D&C 45:39).

We can be pretty certain that the Lord is not suggesting that we look on these things with joy and delight. They will be very troubling in some ways. But for those that know and understand that these catastrophes are signs of the time, given by God to help us prepare for the days that are coming, Jesus promised that we can "be not troubled."

Through the teachings of President Woodruff about the angels described in the parable of the wheat and the tares, we are given a perspective on why the Lord allows these catastrophes to occur. Modern prophets have given similar warnings, even though they may not mention the parable.

Some years ago, President Russell M. Ballard, now the Acting President of the Quorum of the Twelve Apostles, spoke at Brigham Young University and mentioned natural disasters and calamities. After quoting some passages from the Olivet Discourse, he said:

> I would like to discuss a subject that is on a lot of people's minds. My intention is not to alarm or to frighten, but to discuss the significant and interesting times in which we are now living, to consider some of the events and circumstances we can anticipate in the future, and to suggest a few things we can all do to fortify ourselves and our families for the challenges and trials that will surely come into all of our lives at one time or another. . . . Some of these things seem to be occurring with ever-increasing regularity. If you measured the natural disasters that have occurred in the world during the last ten years and plotted that year by year, you would see an acceleration. The earth is rumbling, and earthquakes are occurring in "divers places." Human nature being what it is, we don't normally pay much attention to these natural phenomena until they happen close to where we are living. But when we contemplate what has happened during the past decade, not only with earthquakes but also with regard to hurricanes, floods, tornadoes, volcanic eruptions, and the like, you would see an accelerating pattern. ("When Shall These Things Be?" *Ensign*, December 1996)

Two thousand years ago, the Savior gave us the parable of the wheat and the tares. In our dispensation, through the Prophet Joseph Smith, the Lord confirmed that this parable would start to be fulfilled in our time and day. Today, we are living in times when the prophecies are being fulfilled.

President Russell M. Nelson has frequently spoken of the need to prepare for the Lord's return. Though he has also spoken of various challenges that may come our way, which may include natural disasters, he has also vigorously counseled us on how to *prepare spiritually* for what is coming. Mostly he reminds us of our need to bring more revelation and inspiration into our lives. Here is a sampling of his inspired counsel to us on this matter:

> We live in a time of turmoil. Earthquakes and tsunamis wreak devastation, governments collapse, economic stresses are severe, the family is under attack, and divorce rates are rising. We have great cause for concern. But we do not need to let our fears displace our faith. We can combat those fears by strengthening our faith. . . . Why do we need such resilient faith? *Because difficult days are ahead.* ("Face the Future with Faith," *Ensign*, May 2011; emphasis added)

> I am optimistic about the future. It will be filled with opportunities for each of us to progress, contribute, and take the gospel to every corner of the earth. But I am also not naive about the days ahead. We live in a world that is complex and increasingly contentious. . . . If we are to have any hope of sifting through the myriad of voices and the philosophies of men that attack truth, we must learn to receive revelation. Our Savior and Redeemer, Jesus Christ, will perform some of His mightiest works between now and when He comes again. We will see miraculous indications that God the Father and His Son, Jesus Christ, preside over this Church in majesty and glory. But in coming days, it will not be possible to survive spiritually without the guiding, directing, and comforting influence of the Holy Ghost. . . . I plead with you to increase your spiritual capacity to receive revelation. ("Revelation for the Church, Revelation for Our Lives," *Ensign*, May 2018)

Speaking to the youth of the Church in a worldwide broadcast, President Nelson made this promise: "I promise you that if you will *sincerely and persistently do the spiritual work needed to develop the crucial, spiritual skill of learning how to hear the whisperings of the Holy Ghost,* you will have all the direction you will ever need in your life." Sister Wendy W. Nelson then added: "There has never been a time like this in the history of the world. Never!" ("Hope of Israel," Worldwide Youth Devotional, June 3, 2018, 3, 7).

Through the revelation given to President Wilford Woodruff, we know that the fulfillment of the parable of the wheat and the tares has begun. We do not know how soon these angels of judgment will have prepared the world for His coming. What we do know is how to prepare for it. We do not know whether we will still be alive to see His coming or will witness it from the world of spirits. But we do know how to prepare ourselves and our loved ones for the challenges of these latter days.

NOTES

1. Joseph Smith Translation differences are shown in bold.
2. There was no mention of this in the dedicatory prayer of the temple.

Chapter 14

The Unjust Steward

CONTEXT AND SETTING

Some people have called this parable the most unusual and surprising of all the parables of Jesus. The reason for that is that the main character in the parable is a thief and a scoundrel, an immoral con man whose goal in life is to be rich and who is willing to do anything to achieve and maintain that status. And yet Jesus appears to praise him for his actions.

This parable immediately follows the parables of lost things—the lost sheep, the lost coin, and the lost sons—discussed in previous chapters. Because of that, some have thought that Jesus grouped this steward with the others since he is also a lost soul. But the text gives no hint of that, and there seems to be a different lesson that Jesus shared with His listeners. Luke introduces it simply with, "And he said also unto his disciples, There was a certain rich man. . . ." (Luke 16:1).

What immediately follows the parable may be more helpful in giving us the context than what preceded it. When the parable was finished, Luke indicated that there were Pharisees there who "derided" Jesus for what He said. That was not unusual. He constantly criticized them, and they constantly struck back with bitter invective. In this case, their bitterness may well have come from the fact that they had clearly understood that the parable was a direct criticism of them (see Luke 16:14).

Jesus then further accused them of trying to justify their wickedness, but said that God knew their hearts and warned them that what some men highly esteemed was an abomination in God's sight. He then gave them some examples of their pride and wickedness (see Luke 16:15–18). However, because the parable is really about a steward who willingly uses dishonest means to prepare for himself a comfortable future, I chose to include it in this section, which is on spiritual preparation, for reasons that we shall see as we study the parable.

THE PARABLE

And he said also unto his disciples, There was a certain rich man, which had a steward; and the same was accused unto him that he had wasted his goods. And he called him, and said unto him, How is it that I hear this of thee? give an account of thy stewardship; for thou mayest be no longer steward.

Then the steward said within himself, What shall I do? for my lord taketh away from me the stewardship: I cannot dig; to beg I am ashamed. I am resolved what to do, that, when I am put out of the stewardship, they may receive me into their houses. So he called every one of his lord's debtors unto him, and said unto the first, How much owest thou unto my lord? And he said, An hundred measures of oil. And he said unto him, Take thy bill, and sit down quickly, and write fifty. Then said he to another, And how much owest thou? And he said, An hundred measures of wheat. And he said unto him, Take thy bill, and write fourscore.

And the lord commended the unjust steward, because he

had done wisely: for the children of this world are in their generation wiser than the children of light. (Luke 16:1–8)

Here the parable ends and Jesus comments on what He had just
taught to make sure the message was clear.

And I say unto you : Make to yourselves friends of the mammon of unrighteousness; that, when ye fail, they may receive you
into everlasting habitations.

He that is faithful in that which is least is faithful also in
much: and he that is unjust in the least is unjust also in much.
If therefore ye have not been faithful in the unrighteous mammon, who will commit to your trust the true riches? And if ye
have not been faithful in that which is another man's, who shall
give you that which is your own?

No servant can serve two masters: for either he will hate
the one, and love the other; or else he will hold to the one, and
despise the other. Ye cannot serve God and mammon. (Luke
16:9–13)

ANALYSIS

To begin with, the word "steward" is the key to understanding
the parable. Yet stewards are not found much in modern society, at
least not with that title. It wasn't that long ago that the men and
women who worked on airline flights were called stewards and stew-
ardesses because they served passengers on the plane. But the kind of
steward referenced in the parable would be more like a foreman on a
ranch. His job was to watch over the property and business interests
of his master. He had great responsibility and a lot of freedom and
discretion to further the master's estate. Often he was trusted to the
point that there was not much oversight from his master.

In this case, however, the master had come to suspect that his steward was up to something. This was a deep betrayal of the trust the master had put in his servant, and the suspicious master determined that he would start his own investigation to see if there was any truth in the accusations. The master demanded an accounting. While the steward was shocked and alarmed to find that his dirty little scheme had been discovered, there was not the slightest indication of remorse or regret. Note how Jesus described his response. "What shall I do?" he cried. "I cannot dig. [Heaven forbid!] And to beg I am ashamed." Those two sentences say much about the haughty character and low morals of this man. There is a lot of sorrow and anxiety, but not a pinch of remorse for his fraudulent behavior.

His plan was actually quite brilliant, even though totally immoral. It appears that he had a system for embezzling money from his master, which he had set up with some of the merchants. He didn't take money from the cash box or the master's bank account. Instead, he set up an arrangement with some of the master's clients—some who were themselves dishonest and covetous. It was simple. The steward would falsify the records so they showed the merchants getting a much smaller amount of goods than they actually did. That gave the merchant a large, under-the-table amount of cash, from which he would give the steward a cut. It was slick, and it was profitable for both sides of the deal. And since the merchants already knew that he could deliver what he promised, they quickly sealed the deal with the steward.

What comes next in the parable seems almost shocking. This occurred after the steward was under suspicion. One would expect that the master would soundly condemn such brazen dishonesty and throw the man into prison. But no! Instead, the master actually "commended" the steward because he "had done wisely," as the KJV translates it. Really? Major theft and fraud was praised by the man who had just been robbed?

Here is a case where the translation of the text conveys something to modern readers that it did not convey in the original. In M.R. Vincent's *Word Studies in the New Testament*, he translates it as the lord "admiring his shrewdness, though he himself was defrauded" (1:199).

Even more surprising is that the parable suggests that when the master discovered his servant's perfidy, he didn't take legal action against him, but actually acknowledged that what he had done was very shrewd. Again, that seems odd. Why is there no mention of this crafty steward being arrested and thrown into prison for fraud and embezzlement?

Jesus doesn't comment on that, so we cannot say whether there was or was not punishment. Jesus is making a point about the steward's craftiness in preparing a comfortable living for himself. Remember, the master of a house gave the steward full rights to negotiate with clients directly as he represented the master. Evidently the steward had the right to make these negotiations without consulting the master first. So while he was guilty of perfidy, it appears that he had acted under the authority given him by the master. But that is only a supposition. The Savior didn't address that question in the parable. His purpose was to teach another principle.

APPLICATION

More than one Bible commentator has questioned the authenticity of this parable based on what at first appears to be the Savior's approval of immoral behavior. But here are some things to consider:

- Note that it was "the *lord*," who commended the steward, not "the *Lord*," i.e., not Jesus. But keep in mind who the "lord" or master was. He was a successful businessman, and by extension was likely a rich and powerful man in his own right. In our day, when we hear of men or women who have amassed great fortunes and are admired for their brilliance and success, we are not too shocked when we learn that some also cut more than a few moral corners to get ahead.

- The master commended the servant for his shrewdness, not his dishonesty. Could it be that the master admired his cunning because it was something he might do himself? Again, Jesus doesn't give us any detail on that. But note that the master had every intent of firing him if the accusations proved true. Knowing that it would be confirmed, the steward immediately went into action to ensure himself a comfortable living. And that is what is praised. As Dummelow noted, "The prudence [foresight] of the steward is commended, *not his dishonesty*" (*The One Volume Bible Commentary*, 759).

It appears that one of Jesus's purposes in sharing this parable, especially in the presence of the Pharisees, was to focus on the priorities people set in life, often with no consideration for the future consequences of those choices. The steward may have ensured a comfortable living for himself, but he was very shortsighted indeed, for everyone knows that sooner or later death will come knocking. And those who are wise recognize that with death will come a different kind of reckoning—a reckoning that has eternal consequences. Remember Lazarus and the rich man.

Jesus seems to have been trying to make that clear when He then spoke to His listeners, which included the covetous Pharisees who were there that day. They were doing something very similar to what the cunning steward did. They used their position of power, authority, and influence to make themselves rich. From the New Testament, it appears that next to the Roman leadership, the Jewish religious leaders were some of the richest men in the province. And the irony is, these men who pretended to be the most pious and righteous of them all were much like the perfidious and dishonest steward.

But it is not their dishonesty that the Savior was commending. It was their cunning and commitment to do what their hearts were set on—amassing wealth so that they could enjoy the lifestyle of the rich and famous, which was their great ambition. And, given that value system, what the steward did—and what some of the Jewish leaders were doing—was a "wise" thing for them to do, considering their priorities in life.

Note how Jesus differentiated between the motives of "the children of the world" and "the children of light." Based on the value system of the steward—and the Pharisees—using dishonest means to become rich (i.e., gather in the wealth of the world) was a cunning and successful strategy that helped them achieve their goal.

But for the disciples of Jesus who had come into the kingdom of God believing that this life was not the end, evidently some were more interested in the things of the world—mammon—than they were in preparing for the next world. This is why they were foolish.

In one sense, mammon, or money and worldly wealth, in and of itself is not inherently negative or positive, good or evil. It is how we view it and how we use mammon that determines whether it is right or wrong. Note how Luke sums up what happened that day: "And the Pharisees also, who were covetous, heard all these things: and they derided him" (Luke 16:14). They were not shamed by the parable; only disgusted by it.

In his classic work on the Savior, Elder James E. Talmage said of this parable:

> Our Lord's purpose was to show the contrast between
> the care, thoughtfulness, and devotion of men engaged in
> the money-making affairs of earth, and the half-hearted

ways of many who are professedly striving after spiritual riches. . . . Emulate the unjust steward and the lovers of mammon, not in their dishonesty, cupidity, and miserly hoarding of wealth, but in their zeal, forethought, and provision for the future." (*Jesus the Christ*, 463, 464)

Elder Jeffrey R. Holland expressed it this way as he noted that a common failing of the Nephites was the quest for wealth, and why it often led to their downfall:

> Wealth is a jealous master who will not be served half-heartedly and will suffer no rival—not even God. . . . In return for unquestioning obedience, wealth promises security, power, position, and honors, in fact anything in this world. Above all, the Nephites like the Romans saw in it a mark of superiority and would do anything to get hold of it, for to them "money answereth all things" (Ecclesiastes 10:19.). . . . Along with this, of course, everyone dresses in the height of fashion, the main point being always that the proper clothes are expensive—the expression "costly apparel" occurs 14 times in the Book of Mormon. The more important wealth is, the less important it is how one gets it. (*Since Cumorah*, 393–94)

How would having the kind of zeal for spiritual wealth that Jesus described:

- Change our priorities in this life?
- Affect the consistency and intensity of our gospel study and prayers?
- Influence how diligent we are in serving those in need?
- Change how we spend our discretionary time?
- Influence how we observe the Sabbath day?

These are some of the questions the parable of the unjust steward should raise in the hearts of those who are striving to prepare for the next life as well as this one. As Elder Neal A. Maxwell summed up, using his wonderful gift for words, "Large bank accounts [cannot] fill the empty vault of the soul" (*The Neal A. Maxwell Quote Book*, 413).

Chapter 15

The
Ten Virgins

CONTEXT AND SETTING

In Matthew's Gospel, three parables were given one right after the other (see Matthew 25). Matthew is the only Gospel writer who recorded them. They were given in the last week of the Savior's life, which, as far as we know, makes them the last parables that He taught as part of His mortal ministry. The context for all three parables is the same since they came one right after the other. Though in one way they are three separate and independent parables, in another they are like a trilogy, for their messages are related and support each other.

We shall examine each parable separately, then examine how they are related to each other.

THE PARABLE OF THE TEN VIRGINS

On this particular day in the last week of the Savior's mortal life, Jesus and the Twelve had been on the Temple Mount, with Jesus teaching and mingling with the crowds. Probably later in the day, they were preparing to head back to Bethany, most likely to stay overnight with Martha, Mary, and Lazarus.

The Twelve were mostly from Galilee, in the north of the

Province of Judea, so the magnificent buildings, the columned porticos, and the sweeping plazas of the Temple Mount in Jerusalem filled them with awe. There were commenting to each other on the magnificence and grandeur of the work. It was then that Jesus said something that must have shocked them. "See ye not all these things?" He asked. "Verily I say unto you, There shall not be left here one stone upon the another, that shall not be thrown down" (Matthew 24:2; see also D&C 45:20; JS—Matthew 1:3).[1]

Some of those very stones remain today in what is called the Western Wall in Old Jerusalem. The larger ones are sixteen feet long and weigh close to five hundred tons, so it's not surprising that the Twelve were stunned by His pronouncement. But Jesus walked on without further comment. They left the Temple Mount through the eastern gate and started up the slopes of the Mount of Olives, which lies directly east of the Temple Mount. Before they reached the top, they stopped for a time, probably to rest during the steep climb.

Obviously troubled by what He had said, Matthew recorded that "the disciples[2] came unto him privately, saying, Tell us, when shall these things be? And what shall be the sign of thy coming, and of the end of the world (Matthew 24:3), "or the destruction of the wicked, which is the end of the world" (JS—Matthew 1:4).

Jesus took the opportunity to answer the two questions they asked of Him by giving an extensive discourse about what was coming in their own time and also in the last days before He would come again as King of kings and Lord of lords. This has come to be known as the Olivet Discourse because it was given on the Mount of Olives.

Some indication of the importance of this teaching moment is found in the fact that we have five versions of all or part of this discourse. In those five accounts, there is a lot of repetition, but each version has some unique information, and thus it is helpful to study each of them. They are:

- Matthew: His is the longest and most detailed version (see Matthew 24–25). 97 verses.
- Mark: Much shorter (see Mark 13). 37 verses.
- Luke: Even shorter than Mark's (see Luke 21:5–33). 28 verses.
- Joseph Smith: The Prophet's revision of Matthew 24 during his work on the Joseph Smith Translation was extensive enough that it was eventually published separately in the Pearl of Great Price as "Joseph Smith—Matthew." 55 verses.
- The resurrected Christ: As part of what is now section 45 of the Doctrine and Covenants, Jesus taught some of what He taught that day in Jerusalem. Though the revelation didn't attempt to recapture all that Jesus had previously said, this version has a few details not found in any of the other accounts (see D&C 45:16–75). 59 verses.

Thus, there are a total of 276 verses of scripture that describe this prophetic discourse. That is a clear indicator of how significant the Olivet Discourse is for us today.

As the people of that time strayed more and more from the religion that God had given them through Moses, Jesus gave one last warning of their need for a return to their covenants. And in Matthew's account, Jesus also shared three parables, all with a theme of how individuals were to prepare themselves for the challenges coming. Of special significance is that each of these parables teaches a principle about spiritual preparation. These too were part of the Olivet Discourse.

While the Olivet Discourse is very important scripture, our focus will be on the three parables that Christ added to the end of His discourse. The parables begin in chapter 25 of Matthew. Because these are three simple stories and not a continuation of the prophecies, many people, even Bible scholars, have overlooked the fact that chapter 25 is almost certainly a continuation of the Olivet Discourse. This is shown by Matthew's opening line of chapter 25, which begins: "*Then* shall the kingdom of heaven be likened unto. . . ." (Matthew 25:1; emphasis added).

In this case, the use of the word "then" to start the second part of the discourse is enlightening because, as the word suggests, it connects the prophecies to these three parables. Through Joseph Smith we have even more definitive evidence that chapter 25 is a continuation of the Olivet Discourse.

Joseph Smith amplified what was meant by the word "then" in this context. "Then" could be a nebulous term as used here. *When* is then? The King James Version of Matthew's Gospel gives no indication of when "then" referred to. But in the Joseph Smith Translation of that verse, we do have an answer to that question: "And then, *at that day, before the Son of Man comes,* shall the kingdom of heaven be likened unto. . . ." (JST, Matthew 25:1). The three parables then follow.

That is not to suggest that the parables have no relevance outside of that future setting. Each of the three is timeless in its own way and teaches us principles of the gospel that are eternal. But that Joseph Smith Translation addition also shows that these parables have particular relevance for our time and day, which is "before the Son of Man comes."

THE PARABLE

Then shall the kingdom of heaven be likened unto ten virgins, which took their lamps, and went forth to meet the bridegroom. And five of them were wise, and five were foolish. They that were foolish took their lamps, and took no oil with them: But the wise took oil in their vessels with their lamps.

While the bridegroom tarried, they all slumbered and slept. And at midnight there was a cry made, Behold, the bridegroom cometh; go ye out to meet him. Then all those virgins arose, and trimmed[3] their lamps. And the foolish said unto the wise, Give us of your oil; for our lamps are gone out. But the wise answered, saying, Not so; lest there be not enough for us and you: but go ye rather to them that sell, and buy for yourselves.

And while they went to buy, the bridegroom came; and they that were ready went in with him to the marriage: and the door was shut. Afterward came also the other virgins, saying, Lord, Lord, open to us. But he answered and said, Verily I say unto you, I know you not. (Matthew 25:1–12)

The Joseph Smith Translation made a slight but significant correction in that last verse. Instead of saying, "I know you not," in the Joseph Smith Translation, Jesus says, "You know me not" (JST, Matthew 25:11).

That completed the parable itself, but, as He often did, Jesus ended with an admonition to His listeners, and He did that here as well:

Watch therefore, for ye know neither the day nor the hour wherein the Son of man cometh. (Matthew 25:13)

ANALYSIS

In an earlier chapter, we cited a book by a Christian minister of the Church of Scotland who spent many years in the Holy Land back in the late 1800s. He became intimately familiar with the everyday lives and customs of the people who lived there, and he eventually wrote a book called *Bible Manners and Customs*, which provides many wonderful insights into what life was like in the time of Jesus. One of the things the author described for us was a Middle Eastern wedding before the modern world took over. His detailed description is enlightening to our understanding of the parable we are examining.

> [Middle Eastern] marriages usually take place in the evening. . . . The whole attention is turned to the public arrival of the bridegroom to receive the bride prepared for him and waiting in the house among her female attendants. . . .
>
> During the day the bride is conducted to the house of her future husband and she is there assisted by her attendants in putting on the marriage robes and jewellery [sic].
>
> During the evening, the women who have been invited congregate in the room where the bride sits in silence, and spend the time commenting on her appearance, complimenting the relatives, etc. . . .
>
> As the hours drag on their topics of conversation become exhausted, and some of them grow tired and fall asleep. There is nothing more to be done, and everything is in readiness for the reception of the bridegroom, when the cry is heard outside announcing his approach.
>
> The bridegroom meanwhile is absent, spending the day at the house of one of his relatives. There, soon after sunset, that is between seven and eight o'clock, his male friends begin to assemble. . . . The time is occupied with light refreshments, general conversation and the recitation of poetry in praise of the two families . . . and of the bridegroom in particular. After all have been courteously welcomed and their congratulations received, the bridegroom, about eleven o'clock, intimates his wish to set out. Flaming torches are then held aloft by special bearers, lit candles [or small lamps] are handed at the door to each visitor as he goes out, and the

procession sweeps slowly along toward the house where the bride and her female attendants are waiting. A great crowd has meanwhile assembled on the balconies, gardenwalls, and flat roofs of the houses on each side of the road. . . .

The bridegroom is the centre of interest. Voices are heard whispering, 'There he is! there he is!' From time to time women raise their voices in the peculiar shrill, wavering shriek by which joy is expressed at marriages and other times of family and public rejoicing. The sound is heard at a great distance, and is repeated by other voices in advance of the procession, and thus intimation is given of the approach half an hour or more before the marriage escort arrives. . . . As the house is approached the excitement increases, the bride-groom's pace is quickened, and the alarm is raised in louder tones and more repeatedly, 'He is coming, he is coming!'

Before he arrives, the maidens in waiting come forth with lamps and candles a short distance to light up the en-trance, and do honour to the bridegroom and the group of relatives and intimate friends around him. These pass into the final rejoicing and the marriage supper; the others who have discharged their duty in accompanying him to the door, immediately disperse, and the door is shut. (George Mackie, *Bible Manners and Customs*, 123–26)

That description very closely describes a wedding supper at the time of Christ, and therefore helps us gain a better idea of what was happening. One other note on these weddings has to do with what was called the *betrothal*, or what we now call the formal en-gagement party. This was almost as much of a celebration as the wedding. Usually it took place about a year before the wedding. As in the wedding supper, it was a time of joyous reunion. But at that time, the bride and groom were formally engaged. And while they did not live together and had no sexual relations until the marriage, it was considered as binding as the wedding itself and required a formal "divorce" to end it.

With that background, let us examine the key elements of the parable, which can help us better understand some of what Jesus taught the Twelve that day on the Mount of Olives. We do so once again by using the side-by-side comparisons to consider some of the possible interpretations for each symbol.

The marriage supper	In the Old Testament, the covenant that Jehovah (the premortal Jesus) made with Israel was likened to the joining of a husband and wife in the sacred covenant of marriage (see Matthew 22:2, 4; Revelation 19:7, 9), and being faithful to each other and that covenant thereafter. Worshiping false gods was likened to consorting with prostitutes (see Exodus 34:14–16; Hosea 1–2; Ezekiel 16; 23). In scriptures, the covenant with Jehovah to be His people was likened to the "marriage covenant," with Jehovah or Jesus as the Bridegroom and the covenant people, ancient and modern, the bride (see Revelation 21:12; D&C 109:74). One Hebrew scholar described it this way: "The relation existing between God and the Israelitish people [is] everywhere shadowed forth by the prophets under the emblem of the conjugal union, so that the people in worshipping other gods are compared to a harlot and adulteress" (William Wilson, *Old Testament Word Studies*, 480).

The bridegroom	The Bridegroom is the Savior. The covenants we make with the Father are all done in the name of Jesus Christ. When we refuse to make those covenants, or turn away from God, and we lose the promises connected to that relationship. Elder Jeffrey R. Holland made this clear: "The imagery of Jehovah as bridegroom and Israel as bride is among the most commonly used metaphors in scripture, being used by the Lord and his prophets to describe the relationship between Deity and the children of the covenant" (*Christ and the New Covenant*, 290).
The bride	The Church of God. In all dispensations, the Father and the Son have set up an organization called the Church and/or the kingdom of God. This is organized according to revelation from the Father, and its purpose is to carry out the work of the kingdom. In different dispensations, it has taken several forms. In Adam's time, the organization was set up in a patriarchal order (see Bible Dictionary, "Patriarch," 742). 742). Under Abraham, the chosen people were in tribes, then eventually became a nation called the house of Israel. In the Savior's time, He organized The Church of Jesus Christ. In our day we are known as The Church of Jesus Christ of Latter-day Saints, to distinguish us from the early Church. But remember, the covenant is made with

individuals, not an organization, and it is made between the Lord and the people, who are then organized into a formal organization.

The wedding supper

The covenant people joining themselves in a sacred covenant with Jesus Christ, likened to a marriage covenant made at weddings. In former times the covenant took different forms. But as previously noted, it is not just membership in the Church that brings this invitation, but true commitment to the covenant. However, in this parable, the marriage supper also seems to have special application for our day, the last days, prior to the Second Coming of Jesus Christ (see D&C 58:11). At that point, the faithful of all dispensations will be invited to come and celebrate the day of gladness that opens up the Millennium. That will include those who have died and those now living on the earth (see D&C 88:96–98).

The guests

Participation in the kingdom of God is by invitation through covenant, with the expectation that individuals will join themselves to the work of the Lord through covenants— e.g., baptism, receiving the gift of the Holy Ghost, and temple covenants. Dummelow describes them as "professing Christians, who alone . . . are warned of the absolute need of sufficient oil" (*The One Volume Bible Commentary*, 705). In those times, while many guests were invited to the betrothal, only family and close friends were invited to the wedding supper.

The ten virgins

"Virgin," as used in the times of the King James Version, generally referred to an unmarried woman, with the additional assumption that she would be chaste until she was married. Most commentators agree with Clarke, who said that the word "virgins" in this context represented purity and virtue on the part of all present (see *Clarke's Commentary*, 3:237). In another sense, "virgin" suggests that they have not made a "marriage covenant" with anyone else, i.e., they are not worshipping false gods. Wilson said that the Hebrew word translated as "virgin" can include "a virgin just married, a young spouse," and also "a young woman of marriageable age" (*Old Testament Word Studies*, 469). This suggests that virginity conveyed not only sexual purity but also commitment to a present or future spouse. Knowing that the bridegroom, or husband, is the Savior strengthens the concept that the guests also have purity by being true to their covenants. So in a broader sense, the virgins represent all who have made the covenant.

As to whom the ten virgins represent, Spencer W. Kimball, twelfth President of The Church of Jesus Christ of Latter-day Saints said this: "I believe that *the Ten Virgins represent the people of the Church of Jesus Christ and not the rank and file of the world.* All of the virgins, wise and foolish, had accepted the invitation to the wedding supper; they had knowledge of the program and had been warned of the important day to come. They were not the gentiles or the heathens or the pagans, nor were they necessarily corrupt and reprobate, but *they were knowing people who were foolishly unprepared for the vital happenings that were to affect their eternal lives"* (*Faith Precedes the Miracle*, 253–54; emphasis added).

Five foolish virgins

Clarke notes that the word translated as "foolish" here is *moros*, a Greek word that denotes "he who sees not what is proper or necessary" (Clarke, 3:237). To us, "foolish" may denote that the five foolish virgins had simply forgotten to bring extra oil, while *moros* suggests that they didn't forget to get it; they just didn't think having extra oil was that important. That is a significant difference and gives a different insight into who constitutes the five foolish ones.

The lamps

Lamps were used to provide light in times of darkness in a world without electricity. In the time of Christ, there were larger lamps used inside the house and smaller ones that were carried on the palm of the hand when going out at night. Someone described these small, hand lamps as the "flashlights" of the ancient world. Due to their small size, they held only

enough oil to burn for about an hour. They
were made from clay, which was shaped by
hand, and then fired in a kiln to harden the
clay permanently. They were hollow so they
could be filled with oil. One end was pinched
and a small hole made in the clay. Once it was
baked, a wick was laid in the hole so that one
end of it was in the oil and the other in the
air. This end was lit. For our purposes here,
we need to remember that lamps are not the
source of the light, but merely transport
the light.

The oil

Clearly, while the lamps are very important in
this parable, the oil is a central focus of what
Jesus was trying to teach us. Though Jesus
does not say what kind of oil it was, it is almost certain that it was olive oil, which is still
used today in lamps around the world. While
we may say that it is the lamp that provides
the light, it is more precise to say it is burning
olive oil that provides the light. The lamp just
holds up the light to illuminate a greater area.
This is an important element of the parable.
All ten virgins had been invited to the wedding supper. All ten had lamps, and all ten
had oil in their lamps. The key difference was
that five of the virgins had been careless and
didn't have extra oil. Knowing that a hand
lamp would burn for only about an hour if
the oil wasn't replenished, the fact that the five

unwise virgins didn't bring extra suggests that "foolish" was also an appropriate description of their character. Once again, a Christian scholar from earlier days captures the essence of the importance of the lamps:

"Oil is the symbol of the Holy Spirit, and of inward sanctification. Here it stands for all that is earnest and sincere in the Christian life: secret prayer, faith, humility, charity, and good works" (Dummelow, 705).

The bridegroom tarried

Knowing that the Bridegroom is Jesus in His postmortal glory and immortality, the fact that He tarried, i.e., He didn't arrive at the time He was expected, suggests at least two clear possibilities. After His death and Resurrection, Jesus was taken to heaven, where He still dwells unto this day. That is over two thousand years now. That certainly qualifies as having tarried. But more specific to our time, we are in the latter days, in the days known as the dispensation of the fullness of times. That dispensation opened almost two hundred years ago, and still we are waiting for His second return in all of His glory. Again, Dummelow makes an interesting observation in this regard: "The marriage of Christ with His Church is represented in the parable as taking place *in the world to come*, the betrothal having taken place *in this world*" (Dummelow, 705).

No oil in the lamps	This is the crux of the parable, the primary lesson. When the cry went up that the bridegroom was coming, the five foolish virgins realized that their lamps had gone out and that they had no extra oil. They turned to the five who had brought extra oil and begged for them to share. But those five would not, because they needed it for their own lamps. The foolish ones then rushed out to try to purchase more oil.
The door is shut	When the five foolish virgins returned and found the door shut and locked, they were shocked. When they knocked, crying out, "Lord, Lord, open to us" (Matthew 25:11), his answer must have shocked them deeply: "Verily I say unto you, *I know you not*" (v. 12). *What?* Of course he knew them. They were among the select guests invited to the wedding, so it seems a little puzzling that he would say that. But in the Joseph Smith Translation, the Prophet changed that phrase to read, "You know me not" (JST, Matthew 25:11). The authors of *The New Bible Commentary: Revised* summarized the foolishness of the five unprepared virgins and all others who fit into that category: "Spiritual preparation is not something which can be distributed round in a crisis, and the wise are not being selfish but realistic when they point this out. The foolish were shut out because the bridegroom did not know them in a personal way" (846).

APPLICATION

There is so much to be learned from this amazing and thought-provoking parable.

Since the oil—almost certainly olive oil—is the critical element in the parable, a good question for us to address is what oil is meant to represent in our lives. Fortunately, we do not have to speculate on its interpretation. Though neither Matthew's account nor the Joseph Smith Translation tells us what the oil represents, in Doctrine and Covenants section 45, we are told very clearly what the oil represents:

> "At that day, when I shall come in my glory, shall the parable be fulfilled which I spake concerning the ten virgins. For they that are wise and have received the truth, and *have taken the Holy Spirit for their guide*, and have not been deceived—verily I say unto you, they shall not be hewn down and cast into the fire, but shall abide the day." (D&C 45:56–57; emphasis added)

It couldn't be stated much plainer than that: *The oil in our lamps represents the enlightening influence of the Holy Ghost and all of the gifts, powers, and privileges connected with the Spirit of God.* It is an apt metaphor, for the lamps provide light when the olive oil is lit. The gospel is filled with light and truth, which we receive through the gift and power of the Holy Ghost or the Light of Christ.

President Kimball, as quoted above, believed that the ten virgins do not represent the whole world, but specifically members of The Church of Jesus Christ of Latter-day Saints. President Joseph Fielding Smith expressed the same idea:

> Who do you think is going to be saved in the kingdom of God? Well, according to the revelation of the Lord—not over half the members of the Church. When I think of the

parable of the ten virgins—and *that has reference to The
Church of Jesus Christ of Latter-day Saints*, the kingdom of
God, speaking of the last days, the time of his coming—*the
Lord indicates that about half of them will be ready*. When I
see the activities of some of the members of the Church,
I wonder if even half of them will be ready when the Lord
comes. (*Take Heed to Yourselves*, vi; emphasis added)

That is a chilling statistic.

To say that all ten virgins represent Church members is very
enlightening and also very sobering, for it suggests that those who
have accepted the covenant and have strived to be faithful in the
requirements of that covenant will have incredibly wonderful experiences at His coming. There is no indication that these were wicked
and evil people. As noted earlier, their fault was in foolishness, not
wickedness. Remember that it was the Bridegroom Himself, Jesus
the Christ, our Savior and Redeemer, who told the foolish virgins:
"You never knew me" (JST, Matthew 25:12).

President Kimball continues his exploration of this remarkable
parable:

Hundreds of thousands of us today are in this position.
Confidence has been dulled and patience worn thin. It is so
hard to wait and be prepared always. But we cannot allow
ourselves to slumber. The Lord has given us this parable as a
special warning. At midnight, the vital cry was made. . . . At
midnight! Precisely at the darkest hour, when least expected,
the bridegroom came. When the world is full of tribulation
and help is needed, but it seems the time must be past and
hope is vain, then Christ will come. The midnights of life
are the times when heaven comes to offer its joy for man's

weariness. But when the cry sounds, there is no time for preparation. . . .

The foolish asked the others to share their oil, but *spiritual preparedness cannot be shared in an instant*. . . . The kind of oil that is needed to illuminate the way and light up the darkness is not shareable. How can one share obedience to the principle of tithing; a mind at peace from righteous living; an accumulation of knowledge? How can one share faith or testimony? How can one share attitudes or chastity, or the experience of a mission? How can one share temple privileges? *Each must obtain that kind of oil for himself*. . . .

In the parable, oil can be purchased at the market. In our lives *the oil of preparedness is accumulated drop by drop in righteous living*. Attendance at sacrament meetings adds oil to our lamps, drop by drop over the years. Fasting, family prayer, home teaching, control of bodily appetites, preaching the gospel, studying the scriptures—each act of dedication and obedience is a drop added to our store. Deeds of kindness, payment of offerings and tithes, chaste thoughts and actions, marriage in the covenant for eternity—these, too, contribute importantly to the oil *with which we can at midnight refuel our exhausted lamps*. (*Faith Precedes the Miracle*, 254–56)

Sister Mary M. Cook, then First Counselor in the Young Women General Presidency, said this of the lesson we learn from the ten virgins:

In the 25th chapter of Matthew, the parable of the ten virgins teaches us that spiritual preparation is vital and must be achieved individually. . . . The time is now for you to diligently apply yourselves to increasing your spiritual knowledge—drop by drop—through prayer, scripture study, and obedience. The time is now to pursue your education—drop by drop. Each virtuous thought and action also adds oil to your lamps, qualifying you for the guidance of the Holy Ghost, our divine teacher. The Holy Ghost will guide you on your journey here in mortality, even when you feel . . . uncertain of what lies ahead. You need not fear. As you stay on the path that leads to eternal life, the Holy Ghost will guide you in your decisions and in your learning. ("Seek Learning: You Have a Work to Do," *Ensign*, May 2012)

As parents and Church leaders, wouldn't it be wonderful if we had some kind of "spiritual dipstick" that we could use to measure the level of "oil" in the hearts and minds of an individual? Especially for our children. We could stick it in their ear, draw it out, and examine it closely, then say, "Yep! He's about a quart low." Then we could take down a quart of oil from the shelf and "top them off" as they begin their day. How marvelous it would be if we could go to the nearest store and buy a dozen cans of "light and truth" to have on the shelf along with our food storage.

But it does not work that way. In one of the early revelations of this dispensation, Jesus made it very clear that just being a member of the Church is not sufficient. He said: "Behold, this is my doctrine—whosoever *repenteth and cometh unto me*, the same is my church" (D&C 10:67; emphasis added). Clearly, just having our name on a membership record of the Church does not qualify us for the richest blessings of the gospel.

One of the implications of this parable in our own lives is to note that the five virgins were described as being *foolish*, not *wicked*. That's an important point to keep in mind. We are not talking about the hard-core wicked of the world, those who deliberately turn their backs on God and everything He represents. On the other hand, the five wise virgins were described as *wise*, but it doesn't say that they were *perfect*. And thank heaven for that.

One way that we add oil to our lamps is through prayer. Jesus told His followers "that men ought always to pray and not faint [give up]" (Luke 18:1). President Howard W. Hunter warned members of the Church about one aspect of prayer that we are sometimes guilty of:

> If prayer is only a spasmodic cry at the time of crisis, then it is utterly selfish, and we come to think of God as a repairman or a service agency to help us only in our emergencies. We should remember the Most High day and night—always—not only at times when all other assistance has failed and we desperately need help. (*The Teachings of Howard W. Hunter*, 39)

President Gordon B. Hinckley taught the same principle using a different metaphor.

> The trouble with most of our prayers is that we give them *as if we were picking up the telephone and ordering groceries*— we place our order and hang up. We need to meditate, contemplate, think of what we are praying about and for and then speak to the Lord as one man speaketh to another. (*Teachings of Gordon B. Hinckley*, 469)

This selfish casualness qualifies as one form of the "foolishness" that dampens our influence with the Spirit and lessens the spiritual light within us.

The five foolish virgins tried to borrow oil—the source of light—from the five wise virgins. One Christian commentator said of this parable that the five wise virgins were the most "un-Christian Christians" in all of scripture, because they would not share their oil with their sister virgins.

But that's the point, isn't it? We can't simply hand over a portion of our light and truth to others. Elder David A. Bednar spoke of the parable of the ten virgins in general conference a few years ago. He spoke of both testimony and conversion, noting that testimony is "a point of departure; it is not the ultimate destination." He then spoke of this parable:

> Please think of the lamps used by the virgins as the lamps of testimony. The foolish virgins took their lamps of testimony but took no oil with them. Consider the oil to be the oil of conversion. . . . Were the five wise virgins selfish and unwilling to share, or were they indicating correctly that the oil of conversion cannot be borrowed? Can the spiritual strength that results from consistent obedience to the commandments be given to another person? Can the knowledge obtained through diligent study and pondering of the scriptures be conveyed to one who is in need? Can the peace the gospel brings to a faithful Latter-day Saint be transferred to an individual experiencing adversity or great challenge? The clear answer to each of these questions is no. As the wise virgins emphasized properly, each of us must "buy for ourselves." These inspired women were not describing a business transaction; rather, they were emphasizing our individual responsibility to keep our lamp of testimony burning and to obtain an ample supply of the oil of conversion. This precious oil is acquired one drop at a time—"line upon line [and] precept upon precept" (2 Nephi 28:30), patiently and persistently. No shortcut is available; no last-minute flurry of preparation is possible. ("Converted unto the Lord," *Ensign*, November 2012)

Elder Bednar then cited an admonition from the Doctrine and Covenants that refers directly to the parable: "Wherefore, be faithful, praying always, having your lamps trimmed and burning, and oil with you, that you may be ready at the coming of the Bridegroom" (D&C 33:17).

The subtitle of this book uses the metaphors of windows and mirrors. This parable is an excellent example of both metaphors. Though it may be somewhat discomforting, it can be highly profitable to hold up this parable before ourselves as if it were a mirror. That gives us a chance to study ourselves and take spiritual inventory on where we are in this question of having the light of the gospel in our lives. Perhaps we can conjure a "spiritual dipstick" and assess what the level of oil is in our lives.

But there is also the greater and grander view that we find by looking out a window on eternity. This means looking for the broader scope and meaning of the parable—for ourselves, for our families, for the Church and kingdom, and for the world. This wider view will bring its own insights and inspiration. Though the parables of Jesus are wonderful teachers for our own spiritual growth, they also provide a window to the greater designs of the Father and Son for Their children.

Speaking to the members of the Church all around the world, President Russell M. Nelson spoke of the challenges that lay ahead of us. At the same time he gave us counsel on how to prepare for those challenges. Think of the concept of windows and mirrors as we read and ponder his counsel:

> I am optimistic about the future. It will be filled with opportunities for each of us to progress, contribute, and take the gospel to every corner of the earth. But I am also not naive about the days ahead. We live in a world that is complex and increasingly contentious. . . . If we are to have any hope of sifting through the myriad of voices and the philosophies of men that attack truth, *we must learn to receive revelation*

[another way of saying light and truth]. Our Savior and Redeemer, Jesus Christ, will perform some of His mightiest works between now and when He comes again. We will see miraculous indications that God the Father and His Son, Jesus Christ, preside over this Church in majesty and glory. *But in coming days, it will not be possible to survive spiritually without the guiding, directing, and comforting influence of the Holy Ghost* [*oil in our lamps*]. . . . *I plead with you to increase your spiritual capacity to receive revelation.* ("Revelation for the Church, Revelation for Our Lives," *Ensign*, May 2018; emphasis added)

NOTES

1. In AD 70, the Roman general who was sent in to put down yet another Jewish rebellion in Judea breached the temple walls and drove out the last of the Jewish resistance. Knowing well that the temple was a powerful symbol to the Jewish people, the general ordered that the buildings on top of the Temple Mount be torn down. When the war was finally finished, the Temple Mount was still there, but no temple remained.

2. The other accounts suggest that all of the Twelve were there for this discourse, but in Mark's account, only Peter, James, John, and Andrew came over to speak to Jesus (see Mark 13:3).

3. The Greek word used here means "to put in order, to make ready, to prepare" (*Strong's Concordance*, 2889).

Chapter 16

Talents

CONTEXT AND SETTING

The context and setting for the next two parables are the same as for the parable of the ten virgins discussed in the previous chapter. As noted there, Matthew recorded Jesus as giving these parables one right after another as a continuation of the Olivet Discourse.

Many students of the New Testament have treated these three parables as if they were independent parables with no specific connection to each other, except for being found in the same chapter. But I would suggest that there is a connection in the messages of all three parables, which we shall see once we have examined each of the three separately. One last minor point as we begin our study of these two parables: Joseph Smith made no changes in the text of either parable. They are as Matthew wrote them.

THE PARABLE

The kingdom of heaven is as a man travelling into a far country, who called his own servants, and delivered unto them his goods. And unto one he gave five talents, to another two, and to another one; to every man according to his several ability; and straightway took his journey.

Then he that had received the five talents went and traded with the same, and made them other five talents. And likewise he that had received two, he also gained other two. But he that had received one went and digged in the earth, and hid his lord's money.

After a long time the lord of those servants cometh, and reckoneth with them. And so he that had received five talents came and brought other five talents, saying, Lord, thou deliveredst unto me five talents: behold, I have gained beside them five talents more.

His lord said unto him, Well done, thou good and faithful servant: thou hast been faithful over a few things, I will make thee ruler over many things: enter thou into the joy of thy lord.

He also that had received two talents came and said, Lord, thou deliveredst unto me two talents: behold, I have gained two other talents beside them. His lord said unto him, Well done, good and faithful servant; thou hast been faithful over a few things, I will make thee ruler over many things: enter thou into the joy of thy lord.

Then he which had received the one talent came and said, Lord, I knew thee that thou art an hard man, reaping where thou hast not sown, and gathering where thou hast not strawed: And I was afraid, and went and hid thy talent in the earth: lo, there thou hast that is thine.

His lord answered and said unto him, Thou wicked and slothful servant, thou knewest that I reap where I sowed not, and gather where I have not strawed: Thou oughtest therefore to have put my money to the exchangers, and then at my coming I should have received mine own with usury. Take therefore the talent from him, and give it unto him which hath ten talents.

> For unto every one that hath shall be given, and he shall have abundance: but from him that hath not shall be taken away even that which he hath. And cast ye the unprofitable servant into outer darkness: there shall be weeping and gnashing of teeth. (Matthew 25:14–30)

ANALYSIS

As we begin, there are two things we need to particularly note that will help us better understand what this parable seeks to teach us.

First, the word *talent* can be confusing to modern readers because the primary meaning of the word today relates to a person's skills and abilities, their expertise or special aptitude in some field of endeavor or another. But, as noted earlier, in the time of Jesus, a talent was a form of money determined by weight. The Greek word *talanton* has two meanings: first, it is the scales on which the metal is weighed, and it is also the talent itself (see *Strong's Concordance*, 5342). One talent would be worth approximately $520,000 in our monetary system.

On that basis, here is what the rich man gave to his three servants in current US dollars:

First servant: five talents, or $2,600,000

Second servant: two talents, or $1,040,000

Third servant: one talent, or $520,000

All of these were substantial fortunes at that time. This suggests that these were more than servants who cleaned the home or cooked the meals. They were servants who worked with their master in the management of his estate. Jesus doesn't say why he gave the three of them different amounts, but it seems likely that he saw differing levels of ability and integrity in them and acted accordingly. With that background, let us once again examine the key elements of the parable by laying them side by side:

The kingdom of heaven	The Church of Christ; God's kingdom and His plan
The master	Jesus Christ, our Savior and Redeemer, and by extension God the Father
The three servants	Members of the kingdom, people of the covenant, and especially those called to carry out the work of the Lord. That each is different in abilities and talents describes the human condition.
The journey to a far country	Jesus was taken up at his death into heaven, where He remains until His Second Coming.
Talents	The various gifts, abilities, blessings, and help given to each of us by our Heavenly Father and multiplied or diminished by our own effort and diligence.
Several abilities	To us, "several" suggests numerous or multiple, but the Greek word used here means "pertaining to one's self, belonging to one's self." So these would be what we might call personal gifts, talents, and abilities (see *Strong's Concordance*, 2398).
Different value of talents	Each of us has different gifts, blessings, opportunities, and abilities. Though they may differ widely, all blessings come from the hand of the Lord.
The master returns	This seems to suggest our time, our dispensation, the last days before the Second Coming,

therefore not the time of Christ's mortal ministry.

The accounting

What the scriptures call the judgment; the time when we are called to make an accounting of our mortal stewardship to the Lord. We are rewarded or punished according to the choices we make in this life. One thing of special note: even though the first two servants had received a dramatic difference in the amount entrusted to them, both doubled their gift and both received the same identical commendation. From that we can assume that if the third servant had doubled his single talent, his praise would have been the same as the others.

APPLICATION

The literary structure of this parable is quite enlightening. As noted, that the lord gave significantly different amounts of money to the three servants could suggest that he did so based on his knowledge of their abilities and character. And when it came to rewarding them on his return, each of the first two was commended with the same exact words, but they were monetarily rewarded based on how much they had earned for their master, not equally monetarily.

The parable does not make clear whether the gift given to them was a personal payment or an amount for them to further in the employment of their master. And if both of these servants went on again to double what they were given this second time, we can assume they both, once again, would receive the same praise and reward. This suggests that while the natural gifts and abilities the

Father gives to all of His children may differ greatly, all can be magnified and improved upon. And we can assume that all who do so will hear these welcome words: "Well done, thou good and faithful servant" (Matthew 25:21).

In the case of the third servant, considering what happened with the first two, it seems safe to assume that if he too had doubled his one talent, he would have received that same exact commendation. But he did not. Basically, he did nothing except bury the money so it wouldn't be lost. So he received a double condemnation—one for his lack of action, the other for trying to justify his own lack by putting the responsibility on the master. This is why the master called him a "wicked and slothful servant" (v. 26). The lesson of the parable is that his condemnation was not so much because he returned nothing, but that he *did* nothing. And trying to push off the blame for his brazen failure onto the master only multiplied his duplicity.

The message of this parable has to do with our personal accountability to God concerning what we do in this life with the gifts and blessings that are given to each of us. They may differ significantly one from another, but the promise of the parable is clear: If we serve the Master faithfully using whatever we have, we too shall hear that wonderful praise and promise: "Well done, thou good and faithful servant: thou hast been faithful over a few things, I will make thee ruler over many things: enter thou into the joy of thy lord" (Matthew 25:21).

In our time, Joseph Smith was given a revelation about what the Lord called the "gifts of the Spirit." It is now found in the Doctrine and Covenants as section 46. In that revelation we are taught three key things about the spiritual and temporal gifts that come from God.

1. **Why these gifts are given**. "Seek ye earnestly the best gifts, always remembering for what they are given: . . . *for the benefit of those who love me and keep all my commandments, and him that*

seeketh so to do; that all may be benefited that seek or that ask of me" (D&C 46:8–9; emphasis added).

2. **That the gifts vary a great deal, but all come from God.** "Ye should always remember, and always retain in your minds, what those gifts are, that are given unto the church. *For all have not every gift given unto them,* for there are many gifts, and *to every man is given a gift by the Spirit of God. To some is given one, and to some is given another, that all may be profited thereby*" (D&C 46:10–12; emphasis added).

3. **How to be good stewards with the gifts we are given.** "All things must be done in the name of Christ, *whatsoever you do in the Spirit*; And ye must *give thanks unto God* in the Spirit for whatsoever blessing ye are blessed with. And ye *must practice virtue and holiness before me continually.* Even so. Amen" (D&C 46:31–33).

In modern revelation, the Lord made reference to this parable, though not by name: "But with some I am not well pleased, for . . . they hide the talent which I have given unto them, because of the fear of man. . . . Thou shalt not idle away thy time, neither shalt thou bury thy talent that it may not be known" (D&C 60:2, 13). That clearly is a reference to the slothful servant of the parable.

Elder Ronald A. Rasband of the Quorum of the Twelve Apostles, cited that scripture in "Parables of Jesus," an article in the *Ensign.* After citing it, he went on: "Every person comes to earth as a unique individual. Similar threads may run in families, but each of us has a tapestry all our own. . . . The Lord made it clear that it is not good enough for us simply to return to Him the talents He has given us. We are to improve upon and add to our talents. He has promised that if we multiply our talents we will receive eternal joy."

Elder Rasband then gave three principles for applying the lessons of the talents:

1. Seek earnestly to discover the talents the Lord has given you.

2. Use your talents to build up the kingdom of God.

3. Acknowledge God's hand in your success (see "Parables of Jesus," *Ensign*, August 2003).

In the parable, the third servant tried to justify his slothfulness by making pathetic excuses for why he buried his talent in the ground. He was brazen enough to put some of the blame on the master himself, saying that he was a hard man and so he, the servant, feared to take any risks.

President Spencer W. Kimball noted that some members of the Church use similar excuses to justify why they are not doing more with their talents:

> The Church member who has the attitude of leaving it [the work of the kingdom] to others will have much to answer for. There are many who say: "My wife does the Church work!" Others say: "I'm just not the religious kind," as though it does not take effort for most people to serve and do their duty. But God has endowed us with talents and time, with latent abilities and with opportunities to use and develop them in his service. He therefore expects much of us, his privileged children. The parable of the talents is a brilliant summary of the many scriptural passages outlining promises for the diligent and penalties for the slothful. (*The Miracle of Forgiveness*, 91)

Of this parable, the Prophet Joseph Smith said:

> So it is now. Our Master is absent only for a little season, and at the end of it he will call each to render an account; and where the five talents were bestowed, ten will be required; and *he that has made no improvement will be cast out as an unprofitable servant*, while the faithful will enjoy

everlasting honors. Therefore we earnestly implore the grace of our Father to rest upon you, through Jesus Christ his Son, that you may not faint in the hour of temptation, nor be overcome in the time of persecution. (*Discourses*, 81–82)

Can we not see the direct relationship between having the gifts of the Spirit and serving faithfully in the work of the kingdom?

We close with this simple comment with a profound promise that Nephi wrote as part of the vision he received and recorded in the Book of Mormon: "Blessed are they who shall seek to bring forth my Zion at that day, for they shall have the gift and the power of the Holy Ghost; . . . [for] they shall be lifted up at the last day" (1 Nephi 13:37).

The message is that those who seek to foster the work of the Lord—"to bring forth my Zion"—have a very special promise. They shall have the gift and power of the Holy Ghost. There is some wonderful irony in that promise. We need the gift of the Holy Ghost if we are to build up Zion. If we choose to do that work of building, then we shall receive ever more blessings of God through the gift and power of the Holy Ghost.

In the first of these three parables found in the Olivet Discourse, we are taught that we must have oil in our lamps to receive the gift of the Holy Ghost (see D&C 45:57). In the second parable we are told how to increase our privileges with the Holy Ghost—serve faithfully to build up the kingdom of God through our own personal righteousness.

As we shall see, the third parable of this trilogy talks about a third key for how to increase our spirituality and gain a fullness of the gifts of God.

Chapter 17

The Sheep
and the Goats

CONTEXT AND SETTING

The context and setting for this parable are the same as the context and setting for the previous two parables (the parable of the ten virgins and the parable of the talents). All three are part of the Olivet Discourse given by Jesus just days before His Crucifixion.

There is a question to consider as we come to the third parable in this trilogy. It is this: Jesus gave these three parables one right after the other, with no commentary in between. Does that mean these are three independent parables, each teaching its own unique lesson? Or are they somehow connected to each other in some way that we should be aware of?

We have no definitive answer to that question. But, from all that we know, these three brief stories were given at the same time and as part of the same discourse about what the future held for the Lord's covenant people. That is how Matthew presented them to the world. And while some of the other places where the parables are shared, both in New Testament times and in latter-day scriptures, don't place them together as Matthew did, Matthew's version is generally considered to be the most definitive one. One indication of that is that Joseph Smith's revision of the Matthew text (Joseph

Smith—Matthew) became one of the canonized books in the four standard works.

We shall study this last parable separately, as if it were unique. For in some ways, it truly is unique. Then we shall look at all of the parables as if they were three parts of one grand, divine message.

The last section of this book is titled Preparation for Christ's Coming. The parable of the sheep and the goats definitely fits into that category.

THE PARABLE

When the Son of man shall come in his glory, and all the holy angels with him, then shall he sit upon the throne of his glory; and before him shall be gathered all nations: and he shall separate them one from another, as a shepherd divideth his sheep from the goats. And he shall set the sheep on his right hand,[1] but the goats on the left.

Then shall the King say unto them on his right hand, Come, ye blessed of my Father, inherit the kingdom prepared for you from the foundation of the world: For I was an hungred, and ye gave me meat: I was thirsty, and ye gave me drink: I was a stranger, and ye took me in: Naked, and ye clothed me: I was sick, and ye visited me: I was in prison, and ye came unto me.

Then shall the righteous answer him, saying, Lord, when saw we thee an hungred, and fed thee? or thirsty, and gave thee drink? When saw we thee a stranger, and took thee in? or naked, and clothed thee? Or when saw we thee sick, or in prison, and came unto thee?

And the King shall answer and say unto them, Verily, I say unto you, Inasmuch as ye have done it unto one of the least of these my brethren, ye have done it unto the me.

Then shall he say also unto them on the left hand, Depart

from me, ye cursed, into everlasting fire, prepared for the devil and his angels: For I was an hungred, and ye gave me no meat: I was thirsty, and ye gave me no drink: I was a stranger, and ye took me not in: naked, and ye clothed me not: sick, and in prison, and ye visited me not.

Then shall they also answer him, saying, Lord, when saw we thee an hungred, or athirst, or a stranger, or naked, or sick, or in prison, and did not minister unto thee? Then shall he answer them, saying, Verily I say unto you, Inasmuch as ye did it not to one of the least of these, ye did it not to me.

And these shall go away into everlasting punishment: but the righteous into life eternal. (Matthew 25:31–46)

ANALYSIS

There is no ambiguity or deeply hidden meaning in this third parable; Jesus drew on something from everyday life that was a very common sight in the Holy Land of that day—and still is in many places in the world.

A common site out in the countryside of the Middle East is that of a shepherd—often a younger boy or girl—with a flock that includes a mixture of sheep and goats. The contrast between these two animals is dramatic. Most of the goats are grey or jet black. Their long hair is still woven into the fabric used to make Bedouin tents. On the other hand, most of the sheep are white or light brown in color, dramatically distinguishing them from the goats.

Sheep and goats typically grazed together during the day under the watchful eye of the shepherd, but at night they were usually separated. This is because sheep are much more vulnerable to wandering off in the darkness or being attacked by dogs, wolves, or other predators. So the shepherd would put the sheep in an enclosed place called a "sheepfold." These often were small caves or circular enclosures whose walls were made of rock. If that was not available, shepherds would throw up barriers of thick thistles. For shepherds with small flocks that was not a difficult task. Whatever the construction, in all cases, a barrier was placed across the entrance to the sheepfold to keep the sheep in and predators out. In a passage where Jesus Himself said that He was the Good Shepherd, He drew heavily on this imagery (see John 10:1–16).

One gospel commentator noted how often the scriptures draw on this analogy of the sheep and the shepherd:

> The nature of sheep and their relation to man have given rise to many beautiful figures. Jehovah was the Shepherd of Israel, and they were his flock (Psa 23:1; Isa. 40:11, etc); apostasy of sinners from God is likened to the straying of a lost sheep (Psa 119:176; Isa 53:6); Jesus came to earth as the Good Shepherd (Luke 15:4–6). As the sheep is an emblem of meekness, patience, and submission, it is expressly mentioned as typifying these qualities in the person of our blessed Lord (Isa 53:7, Acts 8:32, etc.). (*Unger's Bible Dictionary*, 1009)

Unger also described the goats as having "an unlovely disposition," carrying a bad "stench," and being "stubborn" (*Unger's Bible Dictionary*, 60).

APPLICATION

It is interesting that all three of these parables of preparation speak of inclusion or exclusion, which seems to be determined by one's preparation, or lack of it.

- In the parable of the ten virgins, the lack of preparation on the part of the five foolish virgins led to their exclusion from the wedding supper.

- In the parable of the talents, the third servant's slothfulness—a good term for lack of preparation—led to not only his loss of employment, but eternal consequences as well.
- And in the parable of the sheep and the goats, the consequences that come from the separation are definitely eternal ones—a seat on the right hand of God, or being sent off to "eternal punishments."
- It is especially ironic that in both cases—those who had ministered to the needs of others and those who had not—the individuals were deeply shocked when they were told the basis for their inclusion or exclusion.

This last parable could just as easily have been included in the section on ministering. The contrast between the sheep and the goats is directly tied to that concept. In the section on ministering, particularly in the chapter on the parable of Lazarus and the rich man, there was a long list of admonitions found in the scriptures that counsel us to reach out to those in need, especially the poor, the widows, and the orphans. That the Lord should give us so much direction in this area of service says much about how strongly the Father and the Son feel about us caring for others.

As we ponder on that, it seems clear that there is a dual purpose in the charge to all of the disciples of Jesus. In reaching out and blessing those in need, we lift and cheer and relieve the burdens of others. That is a noble thing. But the scriptures teach us that in ministering service we ourselves are blessed as well, not only in this life but in the life to come. It is a wonderful example of a principle taught in the Doctrine and Covenants, which is that in living the gospel, both the giver and the receiver "are edified" (D&C 50:22).

The message of the parable of the sheep and the goats is so plainly given that we don't need to examine it very vigorously to derive its main message. The goats ignored those in need; the sheep ministered to them.

But, there is something else about these three parables that is intriguing. Jesus gave them one right after the other as He finished the Olivet Discourse. And He gave them without any explanation of why He included them; nor did He expound further on any one of the three. As Matthew recorded them, they are just there at the end of this profound discourse given to the Twelve shortly before Jesus's death. Was that just Matthew putting them together as the conclusion to the discourse, or was that Matthew's way of saying that this was how Jesus gave them and that there was a purpose in Him doing so? Did Jesus deliberately choose, as He so often does in the scriptures, to lay these things together, without explaining why He did so? This question leads us to study His teachings more carefully, and when we do so, then greater understanding and illumination comes. We cannot say definitively one way or another. But that is often true in the scriptures. We are left to search, ponder, and pray for deeper, less obvious lessons from His teaching.

Based on the placement of these three parables at the end of His Olivet Discourse, I am inclined to believe Jesus used these three parables to teach us *how to prepare* for the challenging times that would precede His Second Coming. I believe that they are not three separate and independent parables, each with its own powerful message, but a trilogy of gospel concepts linked together for the specific purpose of helping His disciples—then and now— prepare for the day of His coming. (After all, it is not just those who will be living at the time of His coming who benefit from this instruction. Some of those who heard Jesus teach back in His day are still in the spirit world preparing for His coming as diligently—if not more so—as we are.)

Let us look at the three parables as if they are not three individual, unrelated teaching moments, but three related principles of preparation given by the Savior. To do that we shall step back from the details of the parables and try to see their broader message.

The parable of the ten virgins. The primary lesson taught in this parable is a powerful one, and quite unambiguous. The Savior gave us the key to understand what the oil in the lamps represents. The oil represents the gifts and power of the Holy Ghost, including personal revelation. This is the only way we can be fully prepared to join in the wedding supper, which represents the time of Jesus's Second Coming (see D&C 45:57). If we have that oil in our lamps and an extra supply as well, then we shall be part of the great wedding celebration. To put it more succinctly: the oil of the Holy Spirit is *what* we need to be part of the joy of that day.

The parable of the talents. The Savior gave this parable immediately following the first. And at first glance, it doesn't seem to have anything to do with the Second Coming. But the message is clear. The three servants of the king are asked to build up his kingdom while he is off in a far country. He gives them talents to help foster the work. As noted earlier, in the vision given to Nephi more than six hundred years before Jesus came, the Savior specifically told Nephi that it is the gift and power of the Holy Ghost that helps us build the kingdom (see 1 Nephi 13:37). To put it another way, in the parable of the ten virgins, Jesus taught us what it is we need to do His work successfully—the Holy Ghost and all of its gifts and powers. But in this parable, the three servants are not just told to build up the kingdom, but *how* to do it—by having the light and power of the Holy Ghost in their lives, as Nephi taught.

The parable of the sheep and the goats. This final parable also teaches us *how* we get the Spirit into our lives—by ministering to those in need—but it also defines the ultimate *reward* if we do have the Spirit and do the work of the king, or the ultimate *consequences* if we don't.

To put it another way, it appears that Jesus didn't give us three separate and independent parables. Instead, He gave us the key to how to come back to God—have the gifts and powers of the Holy Spirit. He followed with two other parables that teach us how to consistently have the Spirit: labor faithfully in building God's kingdom and minister to those in need.

Each of those supporting gospel concepts includes numerous principles and applications—honesty, integrity, humility, service, sacrifice, consecration, and so on—which constitute the fullness of the gospel of Jesus Christ and the great plan of happiness.

It is interesting that as near as we can tell, these three parables were the last ones given during Christ's mortal life. How profoundly touching that He would give us three simple keys to eternal life and that the need for personal revelation was given first.

President Russell M. Nelson has often spoken of the need for personal revelation in our lives. Here is just a sampling of his counsel:

When you reach up for the Lord's power in your life with the same intensity that a drowning person has when grasping and gasping for air, power from Jesus Christ will be yours. When the Savior knows you truly want to reach up to Him—when He can feel that the greatest desire of your heart is to draw His power into your life—you will be led by the Holy Ghost to know exactly what you should do. When you spiritually stretch beyond anything you have ever done before, then His power will flow into you. ("Drawing the Power of Jesus Christ into Our Lives," *Ensign*, May 2017)

I urge you to stretch beyond your current spiritual ability to receive personal revelation. . . . Nothing opens the heavens quite like the combination of increased purity, exact obedience, earnest seeking, daily feasting on the words of Christ in the Book of Mormon. ("Revelation for the Church, Revelation for our Lives," *Ensign*, May 2018)

[The Lord] needs men [and women] who intentionally work to hear the voice of the Spirit with clarity. ("We Can Do Better and Be Better," *Ensign*, May 2019)

Let us close with a wonderfully simple and yet profound example of how it can often be small and simple things that bring the Spirit into our lives.

Sister Michelle D. Craig, who was serving as First Counselor in the Young Women General Presidency at the time she shared this in general conference, talked about simple things that can bring the Spirit:

As I pray for the Lord to open my eyes to see things I might not normally see, I often ask myself two questions and pay attention to the impressions that come: "What am I doing that I should stop doing?" and "What am I not doing that I should start doing?"

Months ago, during the sacrament, I asked myself these questions and was surprised by the impression that came. "Stop looking at your phone when you are waiting in lines." Looking at my phone in lines had become almost automatic; I found it a good time to multitask, catch up on email, look at headlines, or scroll through a social media feed.

The next morning, I found myself waiting in a long line at the store. I pulled out my phone and then remembered the impression I had received. I put my phone away and looked around. I saw an elderly gentleman in line ahead of me. His cart was empty except for a few cans of cat food. I felt a little awkward but said something really clever like, "I can see you have a cat." He said that a storm was coming, and he did not want to be caught without cat food. We visited briefly, and then he turned to me and said, "You know, I haven't told anyone this, but today is my birthday." My heart melted. I wished him a happy birthday and offered a silent prayer of thanks that I had not been on my phone and missed an opportunity to truly see and connect with another person who needed it.

With all of my heart I do not want to be like the priest or the Levite on the road to Jericho—one who looks and passes by. ("Eyes to See," *Ensign*, November 2020)

NOTES

1. As an interesting side note, in the law of Moses, the right hand is considered to be what some scholars call the "covenant hand." The law specifically required that various rituals of the law be done with the right hand (see Exodus 29:20; Leviticus 14:14).

Epilogue

Mirrors *and* Windows

About the time He had completed the first year of His ministry, the Savior introduced something new to His disciples and the crowds that came to hear Him. Matthew gave us the most detail about this teaching approach that we now call parables. He records that this began abruptly enough that it took the Twelve by surprise, and evidently left many of the people confused as well.

Parables were not something new that Jesus created. Parables are a literary form found in many cultures throughout all of history, even down into modern times. Some are complex stories, others only short vignettes.

Usually a parable draws moral lessons from things or events that are part of people's everyday life—plants and animals, people, experiences from daily living, and many other things. Most of the parables also drew on the rich complexities of human nature for their messages.

Throughout this book I have suggested again and again that the parables of Jesus are brief but brilliant and profound literary gems. Though they were given more than two thousand years ago, the lessons taught and the language used still ring in our minds and hearts with the clarity of steel hitting on steel.

Most important, this simple literary device, when coupled with the hungering spirit of those seeking truth, can teach wise and practical lessons, but also it can open our eyes to the deepest and most significant principles and doctrines of the gospel of Jesus Christ. And when that happens, this becomes a powerful motivation leading the reader or listener to personal introspection, deep searching of the soul, and, eventually, important changes to the heart and mind. In short, these parables can literally become an amazing catalyst for spiritual growth and gospel maturity.

Based on my own experience, I have introduced two similes that capture the nature of these literary masterpieces.

One comparison is that the parables are like *mirrors* to the soul. As we carefully study the parables and hold them up to ourselves, we can more clearly see what we are and what we are not—either or both of these alternatives can be both painful and a growing experience. Mirrors can help us see more clearly what our Father and His Beloved Son want us to see.

Seeing our flaws in this mirror can lead the humble in heart to change, and those changes can enhance our privileges with the Spirit. And through the Spirit, we start to see things even more clearly. We begin to see the same flaws in ourselves that are found in the characters in the parables. While this can be exquisitely painful, at the same time, it can also be profoundly therapeutic.

The second simile flows from the first. As we start to see beyond ourselves in the mirror of the soul, something very important can happen. In these simple and wondrous stories, we find new insights into the nature of God, our Heavenly Father, and His Son, Jesus Christ. Our perception and understanding goes beyond ourselves as our vistas expand and our vision is sharpened. In these times, the mirrors to the soul become windows into eternity. We see with new eyes the vast grandeur of the Father's plan and we find ourselves understanding the lessons of the parables expanding beyond our own comprehension, enlightening our minds.

When that happens, we begin to grasp with deeper understanding the foundation stones of the Father's plan for His children. We begin to sense how profoundly amazing the love of the Father and the Son is, that it truly is Their work and Their glory to bring to pass the immortality and eternal life of man (see Moses 1:39).

Mirrors and windows. Windows and mirrors. May each of us, as we read, study, and thoughtfully ponder these wonderful narratives we call the parables of Jesus, come to see them as both mirrors of the soul and windows into eternity. Perhaps this is why Matthew said of Jesus: "And all these things spake Jesus unto the multitude in parables; and without a parable spake he not unto them" (Matthew 13:34).

Selected Sources

Clarke, Adam. *Clarke's Commentary: The Holy Bible, Containing the Old and New Testaments, with a Commentary and Critical Notes.* Nashville: Abingdon, 1977.

Dummelow, J. R., ed. *A Commentary on the Holy Bible by Various Writers.* New York: Macmillan, 1975.

Fallows, Samuel, ed. *The Popular and Critical Bible Encyclopedia and Scriptural Dictionary: Fully Defining and Explaining All Religious Terms.* Chicago: J. Mitchell Howard, 1904.

Forbush, William Byron, ed. *Fox's Book of Martyrs: A History of the Lives, Sufferings, and Deaths of the Early Christian and Protestant Martyrs.* Grand Rapids, MI: Zondervan, 1967.

Frank, Harry Thomas. *Discovering the Biblical World.* New York: Harper & Row, 1975.

Guthrie, D., J. A. Motyer, A. M. Stibbs, and D. J. Wiseman, eds. *The New Bible Commentary.* Grand Rapids, MI: Grand Rapids Book Manufacturers, Inc., 1971.

Mackie, G. M. *Bible Manners and Customs.* Grand Rapids, MI: Fleming H. Revell Company, 1898.

McConkie, Bruce R. *The Millennial Messiah.* Salt Lake City: Deseret Book, 1982.

The New Testament in Four Versions. New York: Iversen Associates, 1970.

Smith, William. *A Dictionary of the Bible: Comprising Its Antiquities, Biography, Geography, Natural History and Literature with the Latest*

Researches and References to the Revised Version of the New Testament. Grand Rapids, MI: Zondervan, 1972.

Strong, James. *Strong's Exhaustive Concordance of the Bible.* Peabody, MA: Hendrickson, 2009.

Talmage, James E. *Jesus the Christ: A Study of the Messiah and His Mission according to Holy Scriptures both Ancient and Modern.* Salt Lake City: Deseret Book, 1957.

Unger, Merrill F. *The New Unger's Bible Dictionary.* Chicago: Moody, 2006.

Vincent, M. R. *Word Studies in the New Testament.* Peabody, MA: Hendrickson, 1886.